Education Hell: Rhetoric vs. Reality

Gerald W. Bracey

Because research and information make the difference.

Educational Research Service
1001 North Fairfax Street, Suite 500 • Alexandria, VA 22314
Phone: 703-243-2100 • Toll Free: 800-791-9308
Fax: 703-243-1985 • Toll Free: 800-791-9309

Educational Research Service

1001 North Fairfax Street, Suite 500 • Alexandria, VA 22314-1587
Phone: 703-243-2100 • Toll Free: 800-791-9308
Fax: 703-243-1985 • Toll Free: 800-791-9309
Email: ers@ers.org • Web site: www.ers.org

Educational Research Service is *the* nonprofit organization providing school leaders with essential research for effective decisions. Founded by the national school management associations, ERS is the school leader's best source for resources and data to build more successful schools. Since 1973, education leaders have utilized the ERS advantage to make the most effective school decisions in both day-to-day operations and long-range planning. Refer to the last page of this publication to learn how you can benefit from the services and resources available through an annual ERS subscription. Or visit us online at www.ers.org for a more complete picture of the wealth of preK-12 research information and tools available through ERS subscriptions and resources.

ERS e-Knowledge Portal
http://portal.ers.org

Library of Congress Cataloging-in-Publication Data

Library of Congress Cataloging-in-Publication Data

Bracey, Gerald W. (Gerald Watkins)
   Education hell : rhetoric vs. reality / Gerald W. Bracey.
      p. cm.
   Includes bibliographical references.
   ISBN 978-1-931762-85-4
            1. Educational tests and measurements--United States. 2. Educational accountability--United States. 3. Rewards and punishments in education--United States. 4. United States. No Child Left Behind Act of 2001. I. Title.

LB3051.B67 2009
379.1'580973--dc22

                                              2009010104

Author: Gerald W. Bracey
Editor: Cheryl Bratten
Acquisitions Editor: Kathleen McLane
Layout & Design: Susie McKinley and Libby McNulty

Ordering Information: Additional copies of *Education Hell: Rhetoric vs. Reality* may be purchased at the list price of $30.00; ERS School District Subscriber: $15.00; ERS Individual Subscriber: $22.50. Quantity discounts available. Add the greater of $4.50 or 10% of total purchase price for shipping and handling. Phone orders accepted with Visa, MasterCard, or American Express. Stock No. 0760. ISBN: 978-1-931762-85-4.

Note: ERS is solely responsible for this publication; no approval or endorsement by ERS founders is implied.

Table of Contents

About the Author

In the 42 years since obtaining a doctorate in psychology from Stanford University, Gerald W. Bracey has held positions in school districts, state departments of education, universities, and private educational organizations. Since 1991, he has been an independent researcher and writer, specializing in assessment and policy issues.

Bracey has authored many books bearing titles such as *The War Against America's Public Schools, Setting the Record Straight: Responses to Misconceptions About American Public Schools, Understanding Educational Statistics,* and *Reading Educational Research: How to Avoid Getting Statistically Snookered.*

Bracey writes monthly columns for *Phi Delta Kappan* and NASSP's *Principal Leadership.* He writes op-eds for various newspapers and blogs regularly at www.huffingtonpost.com/gerald-bracey.

He enjoys travel, classical music, and food and was a restaurant critic and wine columnist for newspapers in Richmond, Virginia, and Denver, Colorado.

Foreword

It's midmorning and the elementary principal is preparing for an IEP meeting when a piercing noise and flashing lights startle everyone—the fire alarm. Instantly the principal is moving because she knows it's not a drill. In the halls, students and teachers are bustling in lines toward preassigned areas, just as they practiced. About 2 minutes later the building is empty except for the principal and the janitor who are walking quickly though the halls checking for stragglers and the smell of smoke. They find neither.

Just then a second-grade teacher walks through the front doors holding the hand of one of her students. It's Michael. He's an 8-year-old struggling student from a poor family. The principal, teachers, and reading coach know the family well—two of Michael's older siblings have already been through the school. Right now he's clinging to his teacher's hand and his cheeks are stained with tears.

"Michael," the teacher says in amazement, "pulled the fire alarm."

"Michael, why?" asks the principal. Between sniffles Michael shares his story. He is learning to read real words, he is trying real hard, and today, for the first time, he understood the word on the small red box by the door. It said "pull," and so he pulled it. Then he bursts into tears and wraps both arms around the principal's legs. She pauses, then lifts the sobbing boy and hugs him. "I'm proud that you're learning to read," she whispers. Miracles happen every day in public schools.

A seventh-grade girl sings her first solo in the choir; a down syndrome senior gets to play a couple of minutes in a varsity basketball game and *both* teams make sure he scores a basket; a fourth-grader's home burns to the ground and the next afternoon the PTA has clothes, school supplies, and more; a first-grader comes to school hungry everyday and everyday he gets a good breakfast and lunch.

Miracles happen every day in public schools. Those who are inside the schools see it constantly. And yet, many on the outside describe our schools as failing or declining and speak longingly of the "good old days."

For years, Gerald Bracey has cast a beacon of reason that cuts through the fog of misperception generated by the critics of America's schools. In *Education Hell: Rhetoric vs. Reality*, Bracey makes a convincing case for his position: While there is certainly room for improvement, public schools are as good as or better than they've ever been. Dr. Bracey's report on how schools are burning in the flames of misconception is found in Part I. Long-time critics of our public schools may be quick to dismiss the proof he provides, but those who work within our schools as well as supporters will be nodding their heads in agreement. Our hope is that those who too often see only dire headlines about school's failures will gain a better understanding of the issues and so be more likely to reject a simplistic view of school success.

However, Dr. Bracey's intent is not simply to develop a defense against those criticizing schools. By too easily accepting a credo of "what can be measured matters," critics of our schools—and, too often, the public—have accepted misconceptions about our students' progress as well as their standing among the world's children. And, as he points outs, the problem is more than simply a misinterpretation of test data; it goes to the real essence of what schools should be about. Even though qualities such as creativity, leadership, and citizenship cannot be as easily measured as understanding of a mathematical concept, such qualities are also essential to our children's futures.

In Part II of *Education Hell: Rhetoric vs. Reality*, Dr. Bracey reminds us of the importance of "redirecting the fire consuming schools" to a much more important purpose: rethinking the purpose of schools and how they measure success. He does not provide answers. Instead, he provides a strong and thoughtful foundation for transforming conversations about the goals of public education. Key themes in *Education Hell: Rhetoric vs. Reality* could be used to jumpstart a community's conversations about its schools. Or—as a book study for educators—it could provide support for discussion about the growing impact of international competition, the debilitating effects of poverty, the many facets of intelligence, the teaching of character and citizenship, and the foundation needed in secondary schools to prepare students for college graduation. Such conversations—not unfounded criticisms about public education—take us forward on our journey toward better schools.

Gerald Bracey's views are his own and, while some may not agree with everything he writes, we see him as a positive and persuasive prophet pointing us away from inaccurate and unproductive rhetoric and toward issues important to ensuring a high-quality education for every student. Successful schools are not a destination; they are a timeless journey beginning anew every time a teacher says, "Welcome to my class." We're pleased that Dr. Bracey joins us on this journey.

John C. Draper, Ed.D.
Chief Executive Officer
Educational Research Service

Introduction

In her presidential address to the National Council of Teachers of English, Joanne Yatvin contended that the people who designed No Child Left Behind (NCLB) and similar high-stakes testing programs had no understanding of learning, teaching, or human behavior (Yatvin, 2008). I have now decided that Yatvin was wrong: they were not clueless. They had a *perverted* understanding of learning, teaching, and human behavior. A great deal of evidence in the fields of education, human development, psychology, sociology, and cognitive science contradicts their assumptions and pronouncements.

I can't decide if we have been living in Orwell's world or Lewis Carroll's, but it was a world turned upside-down in any case. The Bush administration declared programs must be based on scientific research and, at the same time, declared war on science it didn't like. "Why is science seemingly at war with President Bush?" asked Andrew Revkin, in *The New York Times*. "For nearly four years, and with rising intensity, scientists in and out of government have criticized the Bush administration, saying it has selected or suppressed research findings to suit preset policies, skewed advisory panels or ignored unwelcome advice, and quashed discussion within federal research agencies" (Revkin, 2004).

Bush's science adviser, John Marburger, a physicist, denied the charges. Howard Gardner, a Harvard cognitive psychologist then said, "I actually feel sorry for Marburger because I think he probably is enough of a scientist to realize that basically he has become a prostitute." (Glanz, 2004). "Discontent among scientists has recently verged on insurrection. In late February, more than 60 influential scientists, including more than 20 Nobel laureates, signed a statement saying the administration had disbanded scientific advisory committees, placed unqualified people on other panels and censored reports by others when their scientific conclusions conflicted with administration policies" (Glanz, 2004). An agenda of single-mindedness and loyalty, not expertise and objectivity, has been the hallmark of the last 8 years. The Center for Public Integrity documents more than 125 failures of the executive branch since 2000. In education, these include NCLB, Reading First, and the student loan scandal (Center for Public Integrity, 2008). (Note: the National Center for Public Integrity only began keeping archives in February 2000). When President Obama said during his inaugural address, "We will restore science to it's rightful place...," you could almost hear the collective "Yes!" from scientists across the country (*The New York Times*, 2009).

Then there are the more general educational perversions of the recent years. John Goodlad wrote, "A flourishing democracy nurtures education; education nourishes democratic character" (Goodlad, 1997, p. *x*). When teachers are forced, against their better judgment, to focus on teaching test content to the exclusion of almost everything else, I can only conclude that the high-stakes testing movement nourishes totalitarian regimes. Consider a more democratic approach rendered by Donald Vandenberg:

Historically, education is the transmission of the human heritage in order to maintain and enhance the level of civilization a given society has attained. Anthropologically, education is the humanization of the young that occurs in the dialogue between the generations and that enables the young to attain adulthood and a place in adult society. Sociologically, education is the socialization of the young into societal roles and values believed necessary and desirable for a society's continued existence. Politically, education is the preparation for citizenship in the state or nation. Economically, education is the acquisition of the knowledge, skills, and values necessary for gainful employment and for training in the workforce. Existentially, education is becoming aware of the possibilities of being that enable one to achieve an adult presence to the world as a morally and socially responsible person with one's own value and dignity. Cosmically, education is the journey of becoming at home in the universe. (in Goodlad, 1997, p. 1)

When was the last time you read something about the cosmic related to education? I'm willing to bet it's been a while. As a psychologist, I might want to add that, psychologically, education is the development of intellectual skills, aesthetic awareness, and creativity.

Perusing an article by Sharon Nichols and David Berliner in the May, 2008, *Phi Delta Kappan,* I was stunned on encountering the phrase "love of learning" (Nichols & Berliner, 2008). Wait! I've heard that before! Just not lately. Lately it's all dreariness and fearmongering about "achievement," achievement narrowly defined by test scores. Get it through your head now: In the long run, test scores don't count. In 1987, in a critique of proposals to change the National Assessment of Educational Progress, the National Academy of Education lamented that many of the qualities we value most are extremely difficult to assess (Alexander & James, 1987). And so we give up on them. We measure what we can and come to value what is measured over what is not. In so doing, we throw away most of education. One day, musing on the National Academy of Education's statement, I made up a list, hardly exhaustive, of personal qualities that we either don't use tests to measure or that, for the most part, we can't use tests to measure:

- Creativity
- Critical thinking
- Resilience
- Motivation
- Persistence
- Curiosity
- Inquisitiveness

- Endurance
- Reliability
- Enthusiasm
- Civic-mindedness
- Self-awareness
- Self-discipline
- Leadership

- Compassion
- Empathy
- Courage
- Imagination
- Sense of humor
- Resourcefulness
- Humility

These are qualities that people can exhibit on an almost daily basis. And, at the risk of diminishing my own profession, I note that none of them *require* schools. Schools, of course, can and should work to develop them. There are other qualities that are rarely evoked but are important nonetheless. Daring comes to mind. Phillippe Petit calls it madness. It comes to mind because, as this was being written, NPR celebrated the 34th anniversary of a daring feat. On August 6, 1976, Petit, with no net and no tie-line, walked a tightrope—between the towers of the World Trade Center, then, at 1,300 feet, the tallest buildings in the world. NPR celebrated the mundane-sounding 34th anniversary because it was accompanied by a film "Man on Wire" recounting the stunt. The film won the 2008 Academy Award for "Best Documentary Feature."

Interviewed for "All Things Considered," Petit said he planned to walk between them even before they were built, having seen drawings in a French magazine. "You have to have contempt for established rules if you want to break them. Madness is very high in my list of virtues" (National Public Radio, 2008).

These qualities, not test scores, are my "frame." B.O. Smith used to say he wanted students who were as compassionate as they were competent. I agree, but creativity tops my list for a variety of reasons. You want global competitiveness? Set up situations where kids can develop their creative skills. The World Economic Forum Global Competitiveness Report for 2007-2008 ranks the U.S. as number one in creativity among 131 nations (World Economic Forum, 2007).

NCLB depresses creativity both in kids and teachers. In fact, in a statement I know she has come to regret, then-assistant secretary of education, Susan Neuman said she hoped NCLB "will stifle, and hopefully it will kill (them) [creative and experimental teaching methods]" (Balta, 2002).

Award-winning journalist Fareed Zakaria noticed several years ago that the Singapore test aces faded as they moved into real life 10 or 20 years down the road while the Americans who trailed Singapore badly on the tests outdid them in every aspect of life (Zakaria, 2006). Puzzled, he asked, "Why?" The Singapore Minister of Education responded that there are some parts of the intellect that you cannot test well. Creativity, for example, or ambition. This is where America excels, said the minister. Most of all, he said, American students are willing to challenge the conventional wisdom, even if it means challenging authority. "These are areas where Singapore must learn from America," he said (Zakaria, 2006).

I do believe that the minister spoke a bit disingenuously in his comment about challenging authority. The last thing an authoritarian regime like Singapore wants is a cadre of educated people challenging authority. But more people than just the minister have commented on this characteristic of American students. Retired researcher Keith Baker cited a Swedish engineer as saying that there is no doubt that European students know more when they graduate from high school, but he lives in Los Angeles and wants his children in American schools because American students develop a "spirit" that you don't see in Europe (Baker, K., 2007). An unlikely source, *Wall Street Journal* editorial board member, Matthew Kaminski agrees. Comparing his American school days with his rigid school life in his native Poland, Kaminski wrote, "From primary school through America's unparalleled universities, our schools teach children to think critically better than almost any other [country]" (Kaminski, 2009).

Zakaria also talked to a Singapore father who had lived in the U.S. for a while, then returned to Singapore. The man observed that when his son spoke up in class in America, he was rewarded with approval. If he spoke up in a Singapore school he was considered "pushy and weird." The man removed his son to a private school more along American lines.

This speaking up is so common in American schools we don't even notice it. Amy Biancolli, an American teaching in Scotland for a year found that it took months of "badgering" her students to get them to ask questions or discuss points of view (Biancolli, 2001). They just weren't used to giving their perspective or opinion or asking questions. Of course, if scripted teaching becomes more prevalent, this characteristic of American students could disappear.

And, if scripted teaching does spread, we are in worse trouble. It is no accident that "creativity" tops my list of qualities. It is what everybody talks about in connection with America and Americans. It is why Asian educators visit American schools in droves to figure out how to make their students more like ours. But, as Robert Sternberg has pointed out, "the increasingly massive and far-reaching use of standardized tests is one of the most effective, if unintentional vehicles this country has created for suppressing creativity" (Sternberg, 2006). Importantly, Sternberg notes in the same essay that projects and performances can and should be evaluated in terms of quality and appropriateness to the assignment as well as creativity; "far-outness" shouldn't be the only criterion.

Twenty years after the National Academy of Education's comments, maybe the world is coming our way. Educational Testing Service (ETS) announced that its Graduate Record Exam (GRE) will include a "Personal Potential Index" with ratings by instructors on "knowledge and creativity; communication skills; capacity for teamwork; resilience; planning and organizational skills; and ethics and integrity" (Hoover, 2008). Students need these qualities, ETS said, to succeed in graduate school. They also happen to be precisely the qualities employers say they're looking for (Barton, 2006; Handel, 2005).

The betrayal of America's schools did not begin with *A Nation at Risk* or NCLB. In fact, it began over 50 years ago. It is true, though, that we have been through an exceptionally nasty 8 years of education hell. David Root, principal of Rocky River Middle School in Cleveland, illustrated the dimensions of that hell. After Rocky River earned an "Excellent" rating on the Ohio Achievement Tests, Root typed out a 2-page, single-spaced apology and sent it to *Cleveland Plain Dealer* reporter, Regina Brett (Brett, 2008). According to Brett, Root is:

> Sorry he spent thousands of tax dollars on test materials, practice tests, postage, and costs for test administration.

> Sorry that his teachers spent less time teaching American history because most of the social studies test questions are about foreign countries.

> Sorry that he didn't suspend a student for assaulting another because that student would have missed valuable test days.

> Sorry he didn't strictly enforce attendance because all absences count against the school on the State Report Card.

> Sorry for pulling children away from art, music, and gym, classes they love, so they could take test-taking strategies.

> Sorry he kept students in school who became sick during the test—failing to complete the test means an automatic F.

> Sorry that the integrity of his teachers is publicly tied to one test.

> Sorry for losing eight days of instruction due to testing activities.

> Sorry he took tests into account in making decisions on assemblies, field trips, and musical performances.

Sorry for arranging for some students to be labeled "at risk" in front of their peers and put in small groups.

Sorry for making his focus as a principal helping teachers teach test indicators.

Sorry that a student asked him, "If I don't do well, will you fire my teacher?" (Brett, 2008)

Root heard from locals (not following board policy!) and from educators all over the country. A superintendent in New Jersey offered him a job should he lose the one at Rocky River. A state legislator asked him if did he not think it was a good and noble goal to have all children proficient in reading and math by 2014. Root replied that it was as good and noble as a goal to have all lawmakers obey the law and lead ethical lives by 2014. Noble, but unrealistic (Root, personal communication).

As noted, the descent into hell didn't start with Bush and NCLB. It started, or at least accelerated, during the first years of the Cold War, the late 1940s and early 1950s, and exploded after *Sputnik* in 1957. As we shall see, the U.S. could have had a satellite in orbit over a year earlier, but for reasons to be explained later—and reasons that had nothing to do with the schools—it didn't. The schools took the hit for *Sputnik* and it's been downhill for them ever since.

Plan of the Book

Looking at the burning ruins left in schools over the last 8 years, we should now be looking at NCLB and asking, "What were they *thinking*?" Former assistant secretary of education Susan Neuman has stated that some in the administration saw NCLB as a tool to expose public education and "blow it up a bit" and that some were "pushing hard for market forces and privatization" (Wallis, 2008). Some of us would consider that the ultimate crime in the last half-century.

So what might appropriate education look like? What should we teach? How? Before attempting any tentative answers to those questions, we have to examine how we got to the low state we find ourselves in. If you want to understand our present condition, you need to know the history of how we got there. We have to look at where we are. NCLB didn't occur in a vacuum. In fact, the report of the Commission on Chapter 1 looks very much like it (Commission on Chapter 1, 1992). It only lacks the specifics of what constitutes Adequate Yearly Progress (AYP), how do you specifically and concretely define a failing school, and what kind of timetable should there be for sanctioning "failing" schools?

The Chapter 1 Report, as much as any I've ever seen, testifies to the power of frames as characterized by George Lakoff (Lakoff, 2004). I know most of the 27 commissioners who put the report together and on few of them would I append the label "conservative." Yet it is a neo-con—or neo-liberal if you prefer—

document. The prevailing form of accountability and testing and enforcement with sanctions that are the essence of NCLB also dominate this report (some of the commissioners did write "supplemental statements" taking issue with some aspects of the full report, mostly the narrow definition of accountability and the unworkability of the proposed testing system). Call it a paradigm if you like, or a frame. I prefer the veil of mystification.

In the 1960s, as reports of body counts and lights at the end of the tunnel assured us victory in Vietnam, some of us took to referring to the "veil of mystification" that governments draped over events to keep people from seeing the truth. The use of the veil obscures the true intent and consequences of NCLB, but it clouds the vision of the Commission report, too. It pervades such organizations as Ed in '08, the Alliance for Educational Excellence, Achieve, the Center for American Progress, and the video "2 Million Minutes." It is the lifeblood of the Hoover Institute, the Heritage Foundation, the Manhattan Institute, Heartland Institute, Department of Education Reform at the University of Arkansas, and similar organizations that wreak havoc on public schools.

We first take a historical look at how we went from a system that valued producing good citizens for a democracy to one that worshipped at the temple of high test scores. We should be asking, what were *we* thinking? Next, we perform what might be termed a little statistical judo. Judo is a martial art that uses the opponent's strength against him. We do that with test scores. Although test scores are a wholly inadequate tool to evaluate the quality of education—in fact, they are the principal tools of the betrayal—

we turn them on their advocates to show that they in no way justify the contention that public education in America is in a state of crisis. With Lakoff's concept of frames in mind, I gave much consideration to not writing this chapter. It is, after all, written using *their* frame. But I decided tests are so embedded in the conversation (unidirectional though it be), that a book that ignored them would itself be ignored as irrelevant to the discussion. I decided I could beat them at their own frame.

Next, we take on NCLB. The chapter after that addresses two vicious myths: that we need more math and science instruction in order to be competitive in the global economy and that we have a dearth of scientists and engineers. Then we disprove a more insidious myth: that poverty doesn't matter, that there are "no excuses." Only then can we examine what a decent, humane, exciting educational system might look like.

This book will not cover the preparation of teachers nor the act and art of teaching. Teaching will *never* be a science. Behavioral science deals with groups; teachers deal (or should deal) with individual kids; nothing works for everyone. Alan Roses stunned an audience in 2003 when he told them that 90% of FDA-approved drugs only work for 35-50% of the people who take them. Roses is a vice president at GlaxoSmithKline, one of the largest pharmaceutical companies in the world. He was not trying to put his company out of business. He was arguing for more research on genetic markers that would allow doctors to better tailor their drug prescriptions to individual genetic makeups (Connor, 2003).

The literature about teaching and teacher preparation are far too large and, therefore, this book does not contain a traditional literature review. The book does not discuss the emergence of the privatizers and the role of business and industry in pummeling schools. I have dealt with this elsewhere (Bracey, 2002b) and these topics have been ably and more comprehensively handled by Molnar (1996), Emery and Ohanian (2004), and Shaker and Heilman (2008). This book will, however, explore a few ideas about learning and discuss what purpose schools should serve, closely following John Goodlad's exposition in *What Schools Are For* (1979).

Finally, we return to the past to re-mine the outcomes of the Eight-Year Study, one of the largest and most overlooked educational efforts in the nation's history. The study or, more accurately, studies, examined what innovations were created when 300 colleges were persuaded to give up their usual admission procedures and accept graduates recommended to them by a set of 30 high schools whose administrators belonged to the Progressive Education Association. While the follow-up of the study examined what happened to students who attended college, the real focus of the study was what happened to *all* students (and to teachers and administrators when freed from the tyranny of a university-imposed curriculum).

PART I

Chapter 1:
Pre-*Sputnik*: Non-Test-Based Criticism of Schools

Eighteenth Century

We begin where all chapters on the history of American education begin, with Thomas Jefferson. Jefferson proposed an education system for America that would function as a great sorting machine. All men might be equal in some moral or legal sense, but certainly not in the realm of the intellect. In his 1782 plan for Virginia, he proposed dividing the state into 5- or 6-square mile areas called hundreds and building in each hundred a primary school located where all children living in the hundred could walk to school. The state would cover the expense for 3 years for those unable to pay tuition. A "visitor" would be assigned a number of schools and each year would choose "the boy, of best genius in the school, of those whose parents are too poor to give them further education, and to send him forward to one of the grammar schools, of which twenty are proposed...." (Jefferson, 1782, in Hammon, Hardwick, & Labert, 2007, p. 352).

The plan makes no provision for educating girls beyond the primary school and no provision for educating the children of slaves.

About the third-year, Jefferson commented, "by this means twenty of the best geniuses will be raked from the rubbish annually" (Jefferson, 1782, in Hammon et al., 2007, p. 352). Clearly, for Jefferson "smart" is something you are, not something you get. Shades of NCLB and its proficient left-behind false dichotomy. These best geniuses would receive 1 or 2 more years of education and the best and brightest of these would receive another 6 years of study. Finally, after the 6 or 7 years of additional education, 50% of the group would progress to 3 years at the College of William & Mary (although he believed in intellectual differences, he did not think that wealthy people were more likely to be smart than poor people).

Jefferson did not see schools as instrumental to a vocation. That was for the rigidly class-determined nations of Europe. He would no doubt be appalled at the obsession today with the dreary idea that schools exist only to fit students for jobs. But, as noted in the opening paragraph, he did see schools as a means of picking the smartest poor children for more education at state expense. Affluent families could send their children to school at their own expense for as long as they desired. "The general objects of this law are to provide an education adapted to the years, to the capacity, and the condition of everyone, and directed to their freedom and happiness" (Jefferson, 1782, in Hammon et al., 2007, p. 352). Freedom and happiness. How quaint.

Schooling existed to ensure another Jeffersonian goal: to sustain democratic government.

> In every government on earth is some trace of human weakness, some germ of corruption and degeneracy which cunning will discover, and wickedness insensibly open, cultivate and improve.

> Every government degenerates when trusted to the rulers of the
> people alone. The people themselves therefore are its only safe
> depositories. And to rend even them safe their minds must be
> improved to a certain degree. (Jefferson, 1782, in Hammon et
> al., 2007, p. 355)

Nineteenth Century

In the middle of the 19th century, Horace Mann took Jeffersonian
education a step further: not only did free men need education to
make wise decisions, they needed education to make them morally fit.

> Never will wisdom preside in the halls of legislation, and its pro-
> found utterances be recorded on the pages of the statute book,
> until Common Schools…shall create a more far-seeing intel-
> ligence and a purer morality than has ever existed among com-
> munities of men. (Mann, 1849, in Cremin, 1961, p. 9)

The next generation of education leaders consolidated Mann's
goal. Many of these are not well remembered simply because they
were not pioneers like Mann. The best known of this group was
William Torrey Harris. Born in Connecticut, Harris moved to St.
Louis and became superintendent of schools, later returning east
as United States Commissioner of Education.

He'd probably be better known if he had written more clearly, but
he became enmeshed in the muddy dialectic created by Georg
Wilhelm Friedrich Hegel in *The Phenomenology of Mind*. Ber-
trand Russell once called Hegel the most difficult philosopher to
read. Some of Hegel's obscurantism rubbed off on Harris.

By the end of the 19th century, the life in schools envisioned by Mann and Harris had not materialized as they had hoped. Rural schools built 50 years earlier were deteriorating. Floods of immigrants packed badly lighted and poorly heated urban schools. Superintendents spoke hopefully of reducing class size to 60. The rapidly expanding industrial world criticized the schools' emphasis on intellect and demanded manual and vocational education.

In 1891, Walter Hines Page edited a magazine called *The Forum*. *The Forum* was known for its discussion-starting articles (Jane Addams, Jacob Riis, and William James were among the high-profile contributors). He asked James Mayer Rice, a young pediatrician who had already written critically about public schools in New York and Baltimore, to study the system on a national scale. He was to observe and pay no attention to anything administrators said; he was to talk to teachers, attend school board meetings, and talk to parents.

Rice visited 36 cities and talked to over 1,200 teachers. He spent 6 months in the field, returning in June, 1892. The first installment appeared that October. Lawrence Cremin reports that "Within a month he [Rice] and Page both knew they had taken an angry bull by the horns. By the time the final essay appeared, Rice's name had become a byword—frequently an epithet—to schoolmen across the nation" (Cremin, 1961). Rice found incompetent teachers using awful pedagogy and, said Cremin, "With alarming frequency, the story was the same: political hacks hiring untrained teachers who blindly led their charges in singsong drill, rote repetition, and meaningless verbiage" (Cremin, 1961, p. 5).

We might dub his report, published in a series running from October 1892 through June 1893, the *A Nation at Risk (ANAR)* of its day. Editorials in papers all over the country addressed it and, generally, agreed with it. Unlike the 1983 *ANAR*, which educators greeted with enthusiasm, educators in 1892 dismissed Rice. He wasn't an educator and didn't know what he was talking about. Educators loved *ANAR* because Coleman's 1966 report on the importance of family in achievement had marginalized schools. *ANAR* turned a spotlight on them and, in the glare of this light, surely the money spigot would flow more generously.

Rice's research led him to write *Scientific Management in Education*. We needed a scientific approach, said Rice, because it's the only way we can finally know what's going on and what pedagogy we should adopt. Sound current? Most of the American journalism known as "muckraking" flowered in the first decade of the 20th century. But Rice was ahead of the pack.

Twentieth Century

Interest in public secondary education remained relatively low until after 1910. Until then, most families lived on farms, consumed what they produced, and needed their children as part of the family workforce. Farm productivity was low because only natural fertilizer was available. In 1910, though, a German chemist, Fritz Haber, patented a process for producing artificial fertilizer. Farm productivity soared while the number of farm workers declined and the proportion of the population living in cities grew. Teenage children, no longer necessary to sustain the farm, enrolled in schools in droves (Glass, 2008).[1]

---

1   It was not just the introduction of artificial fertilizer that produced the increases in productivity and school enrollment. By 1917, Henry Ford had a functioning farm tractor. If children were employed during the Great Depression, the adult unemployment rate would have soared even higher.

The criticism of public schools after Rice and before 1957 received less attention. In 1912, Ella Frances Lynch, identified only as a "former teacher," fired this salvo into the *Ladies Home Journal:*

> Can you imagine a more grossly stupid, a more genuinely asinine system tenaciously persisted in to the fearful detriment of over seventeen million children and at a cost [of] over four-hundred-and-three million dollars each year—a system that not only is absolutely ineffective in its results, but also actually harmful in that it throws every year ninety-three out of every one hundred children into the world of action absolutely unfitted for even the simplest tasks in life? (Lynch, 1912)

One wonders where Lynch obtained the 93% figure given that there was no national database to draw on or any national testing program; only about 15% of age-eligible students were enrolled in secondary school; and testing itself was in its infancy. Testing emerged as a professional endeavor only during World War I. But, hey, lack of data has never stopped any public school basher. Lynch went on to write *Educating the Child at Home* (1914) and a series of "bookless lessons for the teacher-mother" books.

Later *The New York Times* jumped into the fray and surveyed college freshmen on their knowledge of history. Its finding:

> A large majority of the students showed that they had virtually no knowledge of elementary aspects of American history. They could not identify such names as Abraham Lincoln, Thomas Jefferson or Theodore Roosevelt...Many students attending southern colleges thought that Jefferson Davis had been president of the United States during the Civil War...Some students believed that George Washington was President during the war of 1812. Others listed for this war include Alexander

Hamilton, John Adams, Theodore Roosevelt, Andrew Jackson, Thomas Jefferson, Abraham Lincoln and John Jay…Most of our students do not have the faintest notion of what this country looks like. St. Louis was placed on the Pacific Ocean, Lake Huron, Lake Erie, the Atlantic Ocean, Ohio River, St. Lawrence River and almost every place else. (Fine, 1943)

The results disturbed the *Times* sufficiently that it placed them on the first page of a Sunday edition, next to its other major headline of the day, "Patton Attacks East of El Guettar."

The respondents were college freshmen. At the time, about 50% of students graduated from high school and fewer than 20% of those went on to college. One might want to rethink 1983's "rising tide of mediocrity" in light of these results.

In regard to students' knowledge of history, little has changed. In 1987, Chester Finn and Diane Ravitch asked *What Do Our 17-Year-Olds Know?* (Finn & Ravitch, 1987). In terms of history and literature, their answer was: not much. They awarded American students "F's" in both topics. A few years later, though, Dale Whittington (1991) compared scores across generations, in so far as that is possible, and found that today's kids knew at least as much as their parents and grandparents. Given the lower dropout rates of the kids (in 1990), Whittington speculated that they knew more than their parents or grandparents (Whittington, 1991). The Finn-Ravitch conclusion could still be correct in spite of Whittington's finding. We didn't know anything then, don't know anything now. That, at least in part, is because history is taught all wrong, according to James Loewen. His book, *Lies My Teacher Taught Me*, begins:

High school students hate history. When they list their favorite subjects, history invariably comes in last. Students consider history "the most irrelevant" of twenty-one subjects commonly taught in high school. *Bor-r-ring* is the adjective they apply to it. When students can, they avoid it, even though most students get higher grades than in math, science, or English. Even when they are forced to take classes in history, they repress what they learn, so every year or two another study decries what seventeen-year-olds don't know. (Loewen, 1995, p. 1)

Loewen points out that African American, Native American, and Latino students especially hate history and that the achievement gap for history yawns wider than for other subjects. College teachers, he notes, mostly like for students to have taken many courses in their fields in high school. Not history teachers. They claim they have to spend too much time disabusing the kids of what they learned in high school.

Loewen claims the texts bore kids, and distort events. He presents two passages. One from an American history text presents Columbus as a poor man and an underdog, struggling to get the Spanish royalty to listen to him. The other was written by Bartolome de las Casas, who opposed the forced labor, land-grabbing, and slavery that Columbus had brought to Haiti. Never heard of las Casas? That probably means you learned your American history from an American textbook. Never heard that the Spaniards hunted Indians for sport and killed them for dog food? Probably learned about Columbus in an American textbook, most of which are devoted to hero building.

Arthur Newman titles one chapter in his book of readings, *In Defense of the American Public School* (1978), "The Always Abundant Criticism." That's certainly true, but the critiques seem to have been episodic until the Cold War started.

The post-World War II critics came with two concerns: some detractors simply worried about the quality of the curriculum and pedagogy and some worried about a Soviet takeover of the world.

The former produced articles and books like Albert Lynd's "Quackery in the Public Schools,*"* Mortimer Smith's *Diminished Mind,* the very influential *Why Johnny Can't Read* (Rudolf Flesch) and *Educational Wastelands: The Retreat from Learning in Public Schools* (Arthur Bestor). Bestor taught history at the University of Illinois and authored his book after becoming incensed by the recommendations produced at a meeting held to present the results of a study of "Vocational Education in the Years Ahead." Arthur Prosser, a lobbyist for the National Society for the Promotion of Industrial Education, had managed to slip a resolution in to the final report from the U.S. Office of Education that sent Bestor into a rage:

> It is the belief of this conference that, with the aid of this report in final form, the vocational school of a community will be able better to prepare 20 percent of its youth of secondary school age for entrance upon desirable skilled occupations; and that the high school will continue to prepare 20 percent of its students for entrance to college. We do not believe that the remaining 60 percent of our youth of secondary school age will receive the life adjustment training they need and to which they are entitled as American citizen—unless and until the administrators

of public education with the assistance of the vocational educators leaders formulate a comparable program for this group.
(U.S. Office of Education, 1945, p. 15)

Sputnik might have been the first orbiting satellite, but Prosser's
resolution on life adjustment sent Bestor ballistic:

Consider for a moment the extraordinary implications of this
statement. Sixty percent—three-fifths—of the future citizens of
the United States, it asserts without qualification, are incapable
of being benefited by intellectual training or even training for
skilled and desirable occupations. If this is true, it is a fact of
the most shattering significance, for it declares invalid most of
the assumptions that have underlain American democracy. It
enthrones once again the ancient doctrine that a clear majority
of people are destined from birth to be hewers of wood and
drawers of water for a select and superior few. (1953, p. 82)

Bestor attained a certain amount of fame (and notoriety) for his
book and for the many critiques it engendered from not only the
K-12 community but fellow academics as well. In late 1956, *U.S.
News & World Report* published an interview with Bestor under
the title, "We Are Less Educated Than 50 Years Ago" (*U.S. News
& World Report*, 1956). For a historian, Bestor made a number of
mistakes, both in the interview and in the book, that one would
think a historian would know to avoid.

His most common error was to ignore the changing population of
public schools. Fifty years ago, in 1906, only about 7% of an age
cohort graduated from high schools. By 1956, the rate had risen
to 60%. Bestor pointed to declining enrollments in foreign language courses, apparently not realizing that increasing proportions

of students staying in school more than made up for the declining percentages. Ignoring the changing demographics of high school graduates led Bestor to make similar errors about the proportion of students in high school taking math and science.

Paul Elicker, then executive secretary of National Association of Secondary School Principals, wrote a rebuttal containing many arguments, some strong, some not so strong (Elicker, 1958). Among the stronger was Elicker's observation that a Carnegie report found that, in 1908, 49% of Harvard freshmen had "conditions." The figure at Yale was 58%. Today, we would call students with "conditions," students in need of remedial courses. In the 1950s, Elicker wrote, there were *no* students at Ivy League colleges with conditions. Elicker also observed that the "scholarless American public high schools" were also the greatest supplier of those tapped for the learned college society, Phi Beta Kappa (1958).

Still, Elicker's rebuttal, written in the *NASSP Bulletin*, didn't reach the masses who saw the *U.S. News & World Report* article. This would be a common occurrence from now on: strong critiques of the schools would get much media attention; rebuttals would get little or none and likely be consigned to learned journals, not the popular press.

In 1953, of course, the specter of a communist-dominated world pervaded every corner of the nation and every aspect of national life. Bestor took advantage of that to emphasize the threat constituted by life-adjustment education and the "interlocking directorate" of false educators who advocated it. He drew rhetorical inspiration from Churchill and invoked Stalin to deliver his message:

> Across the educational world today stretches an iron curtain
> which the professional educationists are busily fashioning. Be-
> hind it, in slave-labor camps, are the classroom teachers whose
> only hope of rescue is from without. On the hither side lies the
> free world of science and learning, menaced but not yet con-
> quered. A division into two educational worlds is the great dan-
> ger that faces us today. American intellectual life is threatened
> because the first twelve years of formal school in the United
> States are falling more and more under the policy-making con-
> trol of a new breed of educator who has no real place in—who
> does not respect and who is not respected by—the world of sci-
> entists, scholars, and professional men. (Bestor, 1953, p. 121)

Those concerned about a Russian takeover worried about "manpower," a term that seems to have been invented at about the time
of World War II. The end of World War II had brought about a
sense that the world was inexorably interconnected and that the
U.S., as the only involved nation not devastated by the war, had to
abandon its historically isolationist policies and play a role.

Various groups saw schools both as a source of manpower and
as the perfect institution for the Communists to try to subvert.
Hitler's use of adolescents in the German Youth Movement was
fresh in many minds. Organizations such as the Committee on
the Present Danger and the National Manpower Council sprung
up. The former stated that "we need not only trained men but
also the most modern weapons….This means we need both a reservoir of trained men and a continuing advance of every scientific
and technical front." In his Congressional testimony supporting
National Science Foundation legislation, the creator of the large
comprehensive high school, James B. Conant, also spoke up for
manpower: "It is men that count. And today we do not have the

scientific manpower requisite for the job that lies ahead" (Spring, 1976, pp. 77-78). (Conant also favored another idea being discussed at the time, the previously unthinkable notion of universal compulsory military service.) More scientists, more engineers—that's what we need to get out of our manpower predicament.

Until this time, manpower needs had been discussed in terms of the colleges and universities and the military. Now eyes turned to the high schools. Central Intelligence Agency director, Allen Dulles, claimed that the Soviet Union would produce 1.2 million scientists and engineers between 1950 and 1960, while a meager 90,000 would emerge from American institutions of higher education (Spring, 1976, p. 34). One wonders, given the many current intelligence failures, where Dulles got his numbers, but America's "failure" in science and engineering continues today as a favorite theme, as evidenced by the recent floating of phony numbers about engineer production in China and India (for debunking see Bracey, 2006b).

The post-World War II schools were not making it. As early as 1952, education historian Edward Knight saw the trend and observed:

> ...As the first half of the twentieth century came to a close, criticisms of American education were perhaps more numerous and sharper than ever before, and there was much confusion in the immense educational arrangements that the American people had established for themselves. The phenomenal growth of education and its apparent success during these fifty years may have helped to explain some of the issues, as well as much of the confusion, in it at the close of the period. Besides, it was very

obvious that the heavy demands upon the schools, and their difficulty in meeting them, added to the confusion. (1952, p. 462)

Readers might wish to consult Jamie Vollmer's list of burdens put onto the schools since 1900 at www.jamievollmer.com/burden. It's mind boggling.

Chapter 2:
Post-*Sputnik*: Criticisms and the Descent Into Test Mania

Into this acrimonious situation, the Russians dropped a bomb, so to speak—*Sputnik*, on October 4, 1957. Americans displayed many different reactions: Senate Majority Leader Lyndon Johnson was panicked; rocket wunderkind Werhner von Braun was furious; President Eisenhower was satisfied, even pleased; and Russian and American scientists were ecstatic. Bestor assumed a told-you-so attitude. The public, greatly assisted by the media, went with Johnson. Writer Tom Wolfe later described the prevailing mood this way: "Nothing less than *control of the heavens* was at stake. It was Armageddon, the final and decisive battle between good and evil" (Wolfe, 1979, p. 57).

World War II

Von Braun did not put his fury on public display. He was ever the politician and diplomat. He had already talked his way out of death twice. In 1944, the Gestapo threw him in jail and planned to execute him for saying he was more interested in using rockets for space travel than for winning the war. Von Braun, with the help of Nazi architect, Albert Speer, talked them out of it. Once he arrived in America, many people wanted to put him and all of his team on trial as war criminals. But that did not come to pass.

In fact, reasoning that America wouldn't put him on trial was precisely what led von Braun to favor surrendering to the U.S. in the first place. To all but the most fanatical, in early 1945, the Axis power had obviously lost the war, at least the European theater. Von Braun figured that Britain was too war-ravaged to back a big rocket testing program and that the British wouldn't be kind to the man who hurled the V-2 at them, killing some 9,000 citizens and wounding 25,000 more.

No one wanted to fall into the hands of the Russians. Surrendering to France was out, too. Von Braun's V-2 factories used 60,000 slave laborers made up in part of people from the French Resistance—one-third of whom died from starvation and being overworked. Von Braun worried that the French would turn him and his team into slaves in retribution (asked why he had not done anything about the situation, he said he was told to shut up lest he end up working in the "same striped pants" [e.g., as a slave laborer]).

As the war wound down, worried that his own *countrymen* might kill him to keep him from revealing rocket secrets to the Allies, von Braun surrendered to U.S. Army private Fred Schneickert. "I told him I'd be back home before he ever saw America," Schneickert said later. "But I was wrong" (Dickson, 2001, p. 59).

The team later applied for citizenship. For a while they were stationed at El Paso, Texas. One night, officials herded them onto city buses. When they filled out their citizenship applications in response to the query, "point of entry," they would write "El Paso City Line."

In public, von Braun explained the Russian success thusly:

> The main reason is that the United States had no ballistic missile program worth mentioning between 1945 and 1951. These six years during which the Russians obviously laid the groundwork for their large rocket program were irretrievably lost. The United States went into a serious ballistic missile program only in 1951….Thus our present dilemma is not due to the fact that we are not working hard enough now, but that we did not work hard enough during the first six to ten years after the war. (*The Washington Post & Times Herald*, 1957)

Von Braun did not mention the squabbling and infighting among the three services to determine who would get to put something into orbit first (NASA, a civilian coordinating agency, would not exist until 8 months after *Sputnik*'s maiden flight). Nor did he talk about how scattered the missile projects were; he later said, "I doubt if you will believe it but the total figure was 119 different guided missile projects" (Dickson, 2001, p. 125).

Nor did von Braun speak of the incredible neglect of Robert Goddard, our homegrown rocket genius who was all but ignored. When Goddard announced in 1920 he had created a rocket that could fly into deep space, maybe even to the moon, a *New York Times* editorial scoffed at the possibility and ridiculed Goddard. Everyone knew rockets were useless in a vacuum. Goddard, said the learned editors, "seems to lack the knowledge ladled out daily in high school" (*The New York Times*, 1920).

The *Times* was silent on its gaffe until July 17, 1969, when *Apollo 11* sent Neil Armstrong, Buzz Aldrin, and Michael Collins hurtling towards the moon. The *Times* referred to its 1920 editorial and said only, "the *Times* regrets the error" (*The New York Times*, 1969).

Sputnik's Final Irony

Von Braun unleashed his full true feelings at Secretary of Defense Neal McElroy, who happened to be touring von Braun's operation in Huntsville, Alabama. "We knew they were going to do it! Vanguard will never make it. We have the hardware on the shelf. For God's sake turn us loose and let us do something!" (Dickson, 2001, p. 16). (Vanguard was the Navy's program and the project officially designated to orbit something first. It got a tiny satellite up in spring 1958. Its post-*Sputnik* failures generated headlines like "Dudnik," "Flopnik," and "Kaputnik.")

Von Braun knew whereof he spoke. He *did* have the hardware on the shelf. On September 20, 1956, his team launched a 4-stage Jupiter-C rocket from Cape Canaveral. After the third stage fired, the rocket was 862 miles in the air, traveling at 13,000 miles an hour. The fourth stage could have easily bumped something into orbit. The fourth stage was filled with sand (Dickson, 2001, pp. 88-89).

The fate of the fourth stage lay in the strategy and thinking of President Eisenhower and his Science Advisory Committee (and maybe a few interservice memos sabotaging von Braun). Eisenhower wanted better intelligence on military activity in the Soviet empire—troop movements, submarine deployment, missile launches—especially missile launches. The initial solution was the U-2, a plane that could fly almost 100,000 feet above the earth and take pictures. But that was not enough. Eisenhower wanted a system of spy satellites. However, he and his advisors also wanted to keep the space exploration program completely independent of the weapons development rocket programs.

In that regard, von Braun's rocket posed some problems. First, the Vanguard was officially designated as the program for the first orbit. If von Braun's team launched first, it could have well led to a court martial. Moreover, the Jupiter-C looked a lot like von Braun's V-2, and its primary purpose was, indeed, to incinerate Russian cities with nuclear bombs. Eisenhower and some of his advisers worried that the Russians might overreact to a potential mushroom cloud passing over their heads every 90 minutes or so.

In addition, no legal precedent existed to specify who owned deep space. Three years after *Sputnik*, the Russians would get lucky and knock Gary Powers' U-2 out of the air from 90,000 feet. Eisenhower could do little more than beg for Powers' return and offer up a couple of KGB agents in U.S. jails. Thus, that height was still considered sovereign Russian air space. If the Russians went first, the Eisenhower administration reasoned, that would establish that deep space was free and international. In reaction to *Sputnik*, deputy defense secretary Donald Quarles said "the Russians have, in fact, done us a 'good turn' unintentionally establishing a doctrine of freedom of space" (Goodpaster, 1957). Eisenhower wrote, "We felt certain that we could get a great deal more information of all kinds out of the free use of space than they could" (Eisenhower, 1965, p. 210).

Sputnik got a very different reaction from a different crowd. It arrived in the middle of the International Geophysical Year (IGY), actually an 18-month period in 1957 and 1958. The IGY involved more than 60 countries in cooperative exploration of the earth, the seas, and space. As part of the IGY, both Russia and the United States were expected to orbit space vehicles. People anticipated the U.S. would launch first. On October 4, 1957, American and Russian scientists gathered for a party at the Russian Embassy. At about 6:00 P.M. word came of *Sputnik*'s launch.

According to journalist Dickson, "The scientists and engineers assembled at the embassy party were thrilled. Cheers rang out. Within minutes, one of the most impenetrable buildings in Washington was putting out the welcome mat to reporters…Vodka flowed…." (Dickson, 2001, p. 13).

Other than just being there, the satellite had no scientific or military purposes. It had no sensors, no cameras, nothing to record any data. Just a machine that emitted high-pitch "beeps" every 0.3 of a second.

The easiest way to launch a satellite is to take it to the equator where one can get the maximum assist of the earth's eastward rotation. That would produce an orbit with the satellite over water much of the time. The Russians launched at an angle that would take *Sputnik* over much of the earth's land mass. Then they milked that outcome for propaganda purposes. Unaligned nations might lean more towards the Soviet Union given its display of technological superiority. When Moscow put out a schedule showing when *Sputnik* would be over various parts of the U.S., it included Little Rock, Arkansas. Just over a week earlier, Eisenhower had sent troops to Little Rock to protect the nine black students who were trying to integrate Little Rock's Central High School. The message was clear: The Soviet Union is the friend of oppressed people wherever they might be.

As noted, most of the public suffered fears akin to those of Lyndon Johnson. According to Dickson, many sermons presented the situation as Armageddon and at least one pastor said "I wouldn't be surprised if He appeared today" (Dickson, 2001, p. 115). Johnson said "Soon they will be dropping bombs on us from space like school boys dropping rocks from freeway overpasses" (Dickson, 2001, p. 117).[2]

This quote actually reveals how little Johnson, and most of the U.S., understood about rocketry. It is much easier to launch a rocket from point A to point B keeping within the earth's gravitational field than to launch it from point A, put it into orbit, and then orchestrate its return back into the atmosphere for a landing at point B. One need only recall the ocean landings of the early orbital flights of American astronauts, which usually splashed down hundreds of yards, sometimes miles, from where boats were standing by to fetch them from the water.

Media Blame the Schools for *Sputnik* and the Schools Never Recover

Thus there were lots of reasons for the Russians to accomplish space flight ahead of the U.S.: Our neglect of ballistic missile development for 6 years after World War II; our too-many-cooks

---

2   Dickson's book contains hundreds of references in its bibliography but, perhaps because he is a journalist, not an academic, the specific quotes I have used are not linked to specific documents in his treatise. I have been able to verify some, such as the Eisenhower quote in the previous paragraph, but not all.

approach once we did get serious; the internecine rivalries among the services; the disregard of Goddard's achievements; and Eisenhower's thinking about long-range space policy.

None of these reasons had anything to do with what was happening in schools. It didn't matter. The scapegoating began almost immediately.

Given Bestor's dire descriptions of the decline of American education over the last 50 years and his predictions of imminent catastrophe, it was logical that, in early 1958, *U.S. News & World Report* brought Bestor back for a follow-up interview on "What Went Wrong With U.S. Schools" (*U.S. News & World Report*, 1958). Bestor laid the blame squarely on Life Adjustment Education. "In the light of *Sputnik*, 'life-adjustment education' turns out to have been something perilously close to 'death adjustment' for our nation and our children....We have wasted an appalling part of the time of our young people on trivialities. The Russians had sense enough not to do so. That's why the first satellite bears the label 'Made in Russia'"[3] (*U.S. News & World Report*, 1958).

This was utter nonsense. Life Adjustment Education was proposed in 1945. Let us ignore reality for a moment and assume that a curriculum was immediately developed and faithfully put in place and taught by 1946. If a student had encountered it as a 9th-grader in that year, obtained a bachelor's degree in engineering, and joined a space team, he would have been about 25 years old in 1957. Hardly an age to pioneer such a program even for the most talented. Even uber-genius von Braun was 32 when he developed the V-2, and 45 when *Sputnik* went up.

---

3   Bestor loved allusions and his use of the Russian symbol, the bear, might well not have been accidental.

Moreover, if we take Prosser at his word that Life Adjustment Education was only for the 60% who were not served by vocational programs and college tracks, it would have by-passed entirely those headed for science, engineering, and mathematics degrees in colleges and universities.

In any case, the usual reality prevailed. A curriculum was not developed and put in place quickly. Two commissions were formed, workshops were held, the movement came under increasingly strong attack, and faltered in the early 1950s.

> For all their fanfare, the two Commissions had come up with precious little in the way of original thinking or new programs; their self-appointed mission was propaganda and implementation…A fusillade of books and articles slammed into the various pronouncements of the Commissions, with devastating effect. The life-adjustment movement quickly disappeared, as much the victim of its own ill-chosen name as of the deeper attacks on its principles and practices. (Cremin, 1961, p. 338)

Bestor blamed a program that did not exist. Even though faulting schools for letting the Russians get into space first (which we know from the comments of Wernher von Braun was not true) does not pass any reality test, it happened anyway. And it happened over and over as social crises, real and imagined, have appeared. The opening sentence of my 2008 email to *New York Times* columnist Bob Herbert reads, "It is still amazing to me how people who are wise and insightful on most topics under the sun go all goofy when it comes to education" (the email is posted at www.huffingtonpost. com/gerald-bracey as "The Myth Machine Marches On"). People will believe anything you say about public schools as long as it's bad, which led me once to write "Education's Groundhog Day" (Bracey, 2005) using the movie's metaphor of a day that happens over and over and only Bill Murray notices, and on another occasion to write "Believing the Worst" (Bracey, 2006a).

Maybe schools are just victim of a more general process, "Quick, Get Me a Scapegoat" to use the title of Russell Baker's April 2, 1968 column, noticed by *New York Times* education writer Fred Hechinger:

> Almost 10 years ago, when the first Soviet Sputnik went into orbit, the schools were blamed for America's lag in space. Last week, in the Senate, the schools were blamed for the ghetto riots.
>
> In each case, the politicians' motives were suspect. Their reflex reaction, when faced with a national crisis, is to assign guilt to persons with the least power to hit back. The schools, which are nonpolitical but dependent on political purse strings, fill the bill of emergency whipping boy. (1967)

Hechinger only describes half of the process. The second half is to never bestow upon the schools any credit for successes. Two years after Hechinger's column, and a mere 12 years after *Sputnik*, America landed men on the moon and brought them home safely. The Russians, despite their superior schools and vaunted technology never managed, in spite of several attempts, to even *hit* the moon. No one suggested that improved schools had anything to do with Neil Armstrong's "One Small Step for Man."

Time-Life

No organization or publication used the whipping-boy exercise more thoroughly and more effectively than *Life*. Its opening lash stung with the March 24, 1958 issue, the first of a five-part series.

On the cover, in red ink on a black background, were the words "crisis in education." Two portraits dominate the cover. One is of Alexei Kutzkov in Moscow. The other is of Stephen Lapekas in Chicago. Alexei looks stern; Stephen appears to have an easy smile.

Inside, we see Alexei conducting complicated experiments in chemistry and physics and reading aloud from *Sister Carrie*. He works on a truck in shop because, even though in a college-bound program, he must take the vocational courses that are part of the curriculum. Alexei is a 24/7 student. In his "off" hours he plays chess to sharpen his mind. He is seen at a concert under a bust of Russian composer Mikhail Glinka. He reads an English-Russian phrasebook en route to a science museum. He plays the piano at a school evening social (little interest in girls yet) and practices piano an hour a day (after completing his homework, of course).

Stephen is a slacker, at least as depicted by *Life*. We see him walking his girlfriend to school and dancing in rehearsal for the school musical. In one of the few academically oriented photos, Stephen retreats from a geometry problem on the blackboard. "Stephen amused class with wisecracks about his ineptitude," reads the text (*Life*, 1958a, p. 32). Seated at a typewriter, Stephen says, "I type about one word a minute" (p. 33). As Stephen and classmates stare into a clear glass jar, the text advises that "A biology exhibit of dead guinea pigs momentarily diverts Stephen...." (pp. 32-33).

I happened to find Stephen by accident. He will not even today speak of his experience with *Life*. It's easy to understand why. Imagine being a high school junior when *Life* reporters comb the Chicago system for weeks and choose you to be on the cover of perhaps the most popular magazine in America and a reporter and photographer follow you around for a whole week and you turn out to be the poster boy for a horrible educational system (*Life* paid Stephen's mother one dollar for rights to the story).

Stephen went on to become a jet pilot in the Navy and then had a long career as a commercial pilot for TWA.

Stephen's son is a writer and has written about his father's experiences in an article and in emails. He described his father as a C student who regarded college the way a golfer might regard a sand trap. He told me that *Sputnik* galvanized his father and he thinks that it was responsible for his father's Navy and TWA career. He thinks, too, that his father's 30-year career with TWA was a means for him to say "Hey, *Life: floss you!*"[4] (personal communication, April 3, 2007).

---

4   On November 3, 2008, as the Supreme Court was about to hear arguments on when or if "the F-word" is obscene, a National Public Radio's "All Things Considered" segment contained a history of "the F-word." Host Robert Siegel suggested to guest Jesse Scheidlowe, an editor of the Oxford English Language Dictionary and author of *The F-Word*, that continuous repetition of "the F-word" was too cumbersome and could be taken as something of a promo for Scheidlowe's book. Siegel suggested that he and his guest substitute "floss." As in "no big flossing deal." And they did that for the rest of the segment. I have used Siegel's verbal convention here.

I have never found Kutzkov. The Russian embassy did not show a lot of interest. I managed to enlist the aid of Anne Garrels, then the Moscow correspondent for National Public Radio. A couple of months later, though, Garrels phoned while on a trip stateside and said that she and her staff had been unable to find any evidence that Kutzkov had ever existed and suggested *Life* made the whole thing up.

This was not out of the realm of possibility in my experience. As teenagers, my friends and I had an adage for Henry Luce publications: *Time* for people who can't think, *Life* for people who can't even read. I did manage to find one photographer credited with the photos, but, alas, what I found was a death notice. The other photographer, Stan Wayman, died in 1973. The author (Jane Estes, uncredited by name and supplied by Stephen's son), vanishes off the radar in the 1980s. Many searches failed to locate her and substantial cooperation from Time-Life officials failed to find any record of her as a living member in their "alumni" files.

Life thought the situation sufficiently dire to surrender two whole pictureless pages to an essay by novelist Sloan Wilson (*The Man in the Gray Flannel Suit*). Much of Wilson's essay rings depressingly modern. It begins,

> The facts of the school crisis are all out in plain sight—and pretty dreadful to look at....People are complaining that the diploma has been devalued in this nation to the point of meaninglessness....It is hard to deny that America's schools, which were supposed to reflect one of history's noblest dreams and to cultivate the nation's youthful minds, have degenerated into a system for coddling the mediocre. (Wilson, 1958, pp. 36-37)

One can almost hear Wilson toying with a next sentence, "Our nation is threatened by a rising tide of mediocrity," but that sentiment would have to wait 25 years before making its debut in *ANAR*. There was no incentive for eager learners here, claimed Wilson. By contrast, "No one in Russia can entertain the dream of leaving school early and making a million rubles as a salesman" (Wilson, 1958, p. 37).

Although he chastises John Dewey for some of the "silliest language ever heard," he writes sympathetically about the goals of progressivism: "There was a basic humanity in these changes [by Progressives] and common sense too" (Wilson, 1958, p. 36). It sounds a lot like many articles about NCLB: the intent was wonderful, the implementation was awful (although some of us, from the beginning, doubted NCLB's true intent, too).

In the end, Wilson takes the argument beyond *Sputnik* and the arms race:

> It goes without saying nowadays that the outcome of the arms race will depend eventually on our schools and those of the Russians. It is just as obvious, if less often pointed out, that the kind of understanding between peoples which some day may perhaps make arms races unnecessary also depends in large part upon education. (1958, p. 37)

Wilson had long been interested in education reform before *Sputnik* and continued to be afterward. He died in 2003.

Wilson dedicated part of his essay to how Russia and the U.S. treated their talented students. Our neglect of the gifted formed the central theme in the third part of *Life's* five-part series. This one focused on a single student, sixth-grader Barry Wichmann in Rockwell City, Iowa. Barry had an IQ of 162 which rendered him a mystery to teachers and parents alike. One of his teachers complained that she had five students with reading difficulties and, therefore, not enough time to attend to his needs. "Barry and I, we just don't run neck and neck," says his father, a piano tuner and outdoorsman (*Life*, 1958b, p. 93). "I've tried and tried to like baseball," says Barry (*Life*, 1958b, p. 95). But he just can't.

Even though taken under reporter Jane Estes' wing, Barry had a tougher road to success than Lapekas. Estes took him to New York and Chicago (her base). Barry remembers taking a lot of tests there and Estes was close to a Science Research Associates (SRA) administrator, so I imagine one goal of the trip was to run Barry through a battery of SRA tests. Someone at SRA, quoted but not identified, said "I don't know what he will decide to be, but whatever it is, he'll be the best." Estes thought he might be happier at a military school in Indiana, but that didn't work out.

His parents moved to Winchester, Virginia, and the high school there was much more accepting of Barry's genius, not least because he led a team to some victories on "It's Academic," an intellectual TV show that tried to determine which of two teams of high-schoolers was the "smartest."

A 1964 follow-up by Estes seemed to portend not only academic success, but maybe even happiness (1964). Barry had just enrolled at the new Santa Fe campus of St. John's College, an institution with a seminar-based "great books" approach to education. Alas, no one had yet diagnosed a condition that afflicted Barry, dyscalculia, an inability to see the relationship among numbers. [5]

Barry couldn't meet St. John's math requirement. That cost him his 2-S deferment and landed him at Camh Ran Bay during the Vietnam War. He became a Lutheran priest, eventually made his way to Berkeley, pastored a church for gays, lesbians, and transgendered people, and ultimately obtained a doctorate in clinical psychology.

Coleman Report

We have noted already that the schools took the hit for the urban riots of the late 1960s, but after the panic over *Sputnik* died down, schools mostly moved from the spotlight. They were assisted in their walk to the shadows by a wrongly interpreted 1966 report from James Coleman and colleagues. The interpretation was often that school doesn't matter. It's all family. What Coleman's report really said was that schools matter a lot. But, *given school,* there appeared to be little variation among them apart from family variables. He also said that if we want to equalize outcomes from schooling, we'd have to spend a lot more money than we had been spending.

An odd tome appeared in 1970—Charles Silberman's *Crisis in the Classroom* (Silberman, 1970). Odd, because on page 18 of this 553-page book, Silberman writes as follows:

---

5   This condition might cause one to wonder about the accuracy of that IQ figure. One gathers from the articles that he has extraordinary language skills and perhaps talents for the theatre as well.

The Educational Testing Service has assembled some 186 instances in which comparable tests had been given to large and roughly representative national samples of students at two different times during the postwar period; in all but ten of these 186 paired comparisons, the group tested at the later date scored higher than the group tested earlier; the results suggest an improvement, on average of about 20%. (1970)

One hundred and seventy-six out of 186? These then-and-now comparisons present enormous methodological and interpretive problems, but 176 out of 186? For educational research, that's true consistency.

So where's Silberman's "crisis?" Probably in the marketing office at Random House, his publisher. "Crisis" is a word that sells books. We had a crisis because our classrooms were "grim and joyless." They were obsessed with "order and control." And they insisted that children display a most un-childlike quality—silence. Silberman did describe some awful scenes, as had Jonathan Kozol *(Death at an Early Age)*, James Herndon (*The Way It Spozed To Be)*, and Herbert Kohl (*36 Children)* before him. All of these books dealt with all- or almost all-Black schools in impoverished urban areas. Speaking with Silberman some years ago, I got the impression that he was focused too narrowly, no matter how wide might be his range of vignettes, on impoverished schools in New York City, where he lived at the time.

Silberman's book could have had a large positive effect had it not been for another misinterpretation of another educational development. Three years earlier, Joseph Featherstone had described the British Infant Schools and the British implementation of open education in a three-part series in *The New Republic* (Featherstone, 1967a, 1967b, 1967c). Featherstone got that ball rolling in this country, Silberman built on Featherstone, but American educators for the most part interpreted open education as open space and the fad died out within a decade, amidst falling SAT scores and calls for "back to basics."

Test Scores Take Center Stage

Note that Silberman reported a study of test scores and then ignored them as an important indicator of school quality. Earlier education critics, too, had ignored test scores and for good reason—there were none that reflected on the nation. Most states did not have state testing programs until the 1970s. The SAT, created in 1926 and assuming its modern form in 1941, reflected verbal and math skills of only a small minority of the population. The National Assessment of Educational Progress was first administered in 1970.

The criticisms of the early 1950s and the post-*Sputnik* era were based on perceptions and fear, not data. What few data existed were often misinterpreted, as in Bestor's handling of declining enrollments in various subjects.

The criticisms were also based on a false perception of decline. Note that Bestor's subtitle was the *Retreat from Learning in Public Schools*. So far as I know, this was the first title that carried the implication that there was some earlier golden age of American education from which the nation had declined. It also seems to be the case in America that when a previously excluded group is allowed in the schoolhouse door, some people perceive that as an indication that the nation is going to hell in a handbasket. After World War II, America had not only the GI Bill that people could use to attend college, but it moved rapidly towards universal secondary education. Bestor's book appeared 1 year before the Supreme Court ruled on *Brown v. Board of Education of Topeka*, ruling legal segregation unconstitutional, and only 2 years before Martin Luther King, Jr., galvanized the civil rights movement with the Montgomery Bus Boycott.

Scholastic Assessment Test (SAT)

The nature of the criticism changed with the arrival of the next report that bore on how well (supposedly) schools were or were not doing. This report was the 1977 document, *On Further Examination* (College Board, 1977). The College Board had noticed the average score on its flagship test, then called the Scholastic Aptitude Test (for a while called Scholastic Assessment Test, the name School Assessment Test only lasted a few years), and now just the SAT, had dropped every year since 1963.

Little noticed was that while the math started to drop from its average of 500 in 1963, the verbal had dropped 22 points to 478 between 1950 and 1963, a divergence in trends that would seem to rule out any simple explanation. [6] By 1976, the verbal was down to 429, the math to 470.

As will be discussed in the section on specific tests, the SAT affected few people in its early years. In 1951-1952, 1,196,500

---

6   My guess is that this had something to do with the GI Bill of Rights which made college available to many people who would not have otherwise been able to attend. While the mathematics section (then called the quantitative section) did not go beyond simple algebra, the verbal section was a heavily literary test.

students graduated from high school and only 81,200 SATs were administered, but in 1976-1977, the figures were 4,239,000 and 1,409,900 respectively (College Board, 1977, p. 4).

The College Board assembled a panel to find the reasons for the fall. And did it find reasons! One paper assembled for the panel simply listed all of the hypotheses that had been put forward to explain the drop. There were 76 of them. Changes in curriculum, in teachers, in students, in the family, in religion, in values, in national priorities, in the economy, and in technology were all brought forward as explanatory devices. Somehow the panel's staff missed my favorite: the radioactive fallout from the national nuclear testing program in the 1940s and 1950s (Sternglass & Bell, 1983; I cite their most recent piece on the topic, but they had been writing on the damaging effects of fallout on cognition since 1971).

For its part, the panel attributed much of the decline to changes in who was taking the test: more minorities, more women, more students from low-income families, more students with mediocre high school records. It did address some curricular changes it thought reduced the intellectual richness of schools, but it also spoke a lot about a "decade of distraction" that included urban riots; recreational drugs; television; the assassinations of Robert Kennedy, Martin Luther King, Jr., and Malcolm X; and such events as Watergate and the Vietnam War. The counterculture did not worship the establishment's version of scholarship.

The public took a different message from the report: high schools have failed. Rice's 1892 reports and *Sputnik* in 1957 had both said to people that the glowing accounts of public schools from public school officials were not to be trusted.[7] The happy rhetoric from school people hid an awful truth.

But neither Rice nor post-*Sputnik* critics could point to "hard" data to back them up. When *Sputnik* flew round the earth, the National Assessment of Educational Progress did not exist. The SAT was stable. Except for the Iowa Test of Basic Skills (ITBS) and its high school counterpart, the Iowa Test of Educational Development (ITED), norm-referenced tests could not provide long-term trend data on school performance. Each time a test was renormed, the 50th percentile was the average score of a student in each grade. It was thus a floating norm. Only for the ITBS and ITED were new forms statistically equated back to old norms. If in 1958 people *had* looked at ITBS-ITED data from Iowa, they would have seen upward trends.

A shift toward using test scores as the ultimate, and perhaps only, instrument to evaluate schools was already in progress when the College Board panel's report appeared. In the mid-1970s, in reaction to open education and Piaget-influenced approaches to education, a number of states had started back-to-basics programs. Virginia provides a telling example of this and also of how the process started to exclude educators.

In 1974, the Testing Service of the Virginia Department of Education tried to accommodate teachers by giving the tests earlier in

---

7   As Shaker and Heilman (2008) observe, there is a more insidious motive behind rejecting educators. "Educators as a group embody an alternative approach to life in U.S. society. For us values such as the 'life of the mind,' 'aesthetic appreciation,' and 'human service' prevail as motivational priorities and succeed in calling into question 'consumerism,' 'property,' 'wealth,' and 'status.'" (Shaker & Heilman, 2008, p. 104). America has not been kind to those with "alternative approaches." Ask any Native American.

the school year than usual. The turn-around time between testing the kids and getting results back to schools was quite long in those days. Computers were large and slow—in 1974, the Apple II, which came with all of 16K of memory, was 3 years in the future. Teachers complained they didn't get the results in time to use them. In 1974, the department administered the tests in September, likely before students had really settled into the year. Moreover, the norms for the tests presumed that they had been administered sometime between mid-October and mid-November. The combination of testing before the norm dates and student unsettledness produced a dramatic drop in test scores, a decline that induced descriptors like "plunge" and "plummet." The media played it hard with scary graphs showing a precipitous drop in comparison to earlier years. The legislature was furious. The next year, the department restored the normal dates and the scores jumped back to where they had been 2 years earlier.

Too late. The legislature had already passed a "basic skills" law. When I arrived as Director of Research, Evaluation, and Testing in early 1977, my mandate was to devise a set of tests to assess the basic skills that had been developed by the Curriculum and Instruction Division. The next year the legislature gifted us with a minimum competency test law as a requirement for high school graduation. Over the next few years some 35 states passed similar legislation. In 1979, the Virginia legislature decided that, to be consistent, the state needed a teacher minimum competency law. Tests were well on their way to educational stardom.

The minimum competency madness was always something of a consumer fraud. The tests failed enough students to satisfy those who had called for them while not burdening the schools with a passel of failing students. In the end, virtually no one was denied a diploma and, at least in Virginia, those who failed could walk across the stage on graduation day and get a "certificate of attendance." The audience would have been unaware of any distinction between that and a diploma.

Still, the minimum competency and back-to-basics movements solidified in the minds of critics, the media—and some parents— the idea that tests, and not teacher-constructed grades, were the objective, scientific, unflinching measure of what students had or had not learned. That idea further cemented into place in 1983 when the "paper *Sputnik*" arrived, *ANAR* (National Commission on Excellence in Education, 1983).

A Nation at Risk (ANAR)

In 1981, desperately seeking to document the terrible stories he had heard about public education, Secretary of Education Terrel Bell had convened the National Commission on Excellence in Education. It was a strategy of last resort. Bell had hoped to find some "*Sputnik*-like event" that would demonstrate to the public how terrible the schools were. Unable to find such, and even knowing that commission reports usually just took up space on a shelf, he still settled for a commission and its inevitable report (Bell, 1988).

This commission played it smart and hired professional writers to produce the final copy. The report was brief and cast in stark, cold-warrior rhetoric:

> Our nation is at risk. Our once unchallenged preeminence in commerce, industry, science, and technological innovation is being overtaken by competitors throughout the world...the well being of its people, the education foundations of our society are presently being eroded by a rising tide of mediocrity that threatens our very future as a Nation and a people....If an unfriendly foreign power had attempted to impose on America the mediocre education performance that exists today, we might well have viewed it as an act of war...We have, in effect, been committing an act of unthinking, unilateral educational disarmament. (National Commission on Excellence in Education, 1983, p. 5)

This rhetoric impressed many people. About one article a day for the next month appeared in *The Washington Post*. *New York Times* columnist, Russell Baker, though, gave the commission "an A+ in mediocrity" for phrases such as "rising tide of mediocrity" which Baker contended wouldn't pass muster in a 10th-grade essay (Baker, R., 1983).

After the opening rhetorical flourishes, *ANAR* listed 13 indicators of how and why we were at risk. All involved test scores, and many were suspect. For instance, "There was a steady decline in science achievement scores of U.S. 17-year-olds as measured by national assessments of science in 1969, 1973 and 1977" (National Commission on Excellence in Education, 1983, p. 9). These "national assessments" were the National Assessment of Educational Progress (NAEP). One of the "principles of data interpretation" that are the organizers of *Reading Educational Research: How to Avoid Getting Statistically Snookered* is "watch for selectivity in the data" (Bracey, 2006c).

The commission's statement above applies only to 17-year-olds and only to science. A skeptic might wonder why they picked only on science and why they picked only on 17-year-olds. An answer might be this: you don't see that steady decline in science for 9- and 13-year-olds, the other two ages tested. Nor is there any hint of a decline for any of the three ages in reading or math. Thus the commission had nine trend lines—three ages by three subjects—only one of which could be used to support crisis rhetoric. And that was the only one used.

If the commission's rhetoric rang out as revolutionary, its recommendations sanctified the mundane and can be summarized in a word, "more"—more hours in the school day; more days in the school year; more science, math, foreign language courses; more homework; more teachers; more well-trained teachers; more free time for teachers to teach.

The recommendations, incidentally, were directed to school districts and state legislatures. The document did not recommend any federal action. Bell's mandate from President Reagan, after all, was to abolish the federal department of education.

Even so, *ANAR* caused quite a schism in the White House. Adviser Ed Meese and other conservatives urged Reagan not to sign it. Reagan's education agenda consisted of vouchers, tuition tax credits, restoring school prayer, and abolishing the federal Department of Education. *ANAR* addressed none of these. Moderates Mike Deaver and James Baker granted that it did not mention any Reagan agenda items, but advised him to sign the document anyway because it contained much to campaign on.

The above is my summary based on reports of the day and Bell's book. However, Gerry Holton, the most active member of the commission, wrote in *The Chronicle of Higher Education*, on the 20th anniversary of the report, "commissioners...remarked that Reagan was still deciding which of two speeches to give: one by Jim Baker, his chief of staff, and Mike Deaver, deputy chief of staff, who basically supported the report, or the other by Ed Meese, counselor to the president, who was virulently against it" (Holton, 2003).

The day before the report's ceremonial release, Bell received a phone call telling him that Reagan's speech would address vouchers, the value of private schools, and that other evil empire, the National Education Association (NEA). The next morning, Bell called Jim Baker who later assured him that the remarks had been stricken. But when Reagan spoke, he barely mentioned the report. "I looked into the foyer," said Bell. "Ed Meese was standing there with a big smile on his face" (Bell, 1988).

ANAR is still very much part of the daily currency of educators, whether they hate it or consider it a "landmark" report. Consider the use of this paraphrase to describe the 2008 economic crisis:

> We feel compelled to report to the American people that the business and financial foundations of our society are presently being eroded by a rising tide of mediocrity that threatens our very future as a Nation and a people. What was unimaginable a generation ago has begun to occur—companies that extolled themselves as models of excellent practices have deceived the American people with sloppy, undisciplined, and greedy practices that are driving Americans out of their homes, threatening their retirements, and dashing their hopes of a financially secure

future. Indeed, if an unfriendly foreign power had attempted to impose on America the mediocre corporate financial performance that exists today, we might well have viewed it as an act of war. (Glickman, 2008)

ANAR left the school system intact and structured as it had been before the commission rendered its verdict. It did call for a few new practices, such as having veteran teachers mentor newcomers. Soon, though, terms like "indicators of quality," "standards," and "effective schools" appeared. Reagan had advocated vouchers and tuition tax credits, and these were brought forward as means to solving the new "crisis in education." And another new approach to the school system began shortly after Al Shanker, president of the American Federation of Teachers, supported a concept known as "charter schools" first in a speech and then in one of his weekly columns/advertisements in *The New York Times*.

The word "contract" can be substituted for charter with no loss of meaning. The charter freed the schools from some of the alleged onerous rules and regulations. And what did the school offer in return? Improved achievement. How would we know? Test scores, what else?

In his 1996 book on charters, *Charter Schools: Creating Hope and Opportunity for American Education*, advocate Joe Nathan of the University of Minnesota frames the thesis starkly:

> Hundreds of charter schools have been created around this nation by educators who are willing to put their jobs on the line to say, "If we can't improve student achievement, close down our school. This is accountability—clear, specific and real." (1996, p. *xxx*)

And, virtually nonexistent. If what we might call The Nathan Test had been applied to charter schools, precious few of them would be around today. Many *are* around today because the charter issuers were sloppy and it wasn't clear what the charter schools needed to do to meet the charters' requirements; because the charter school evaluators were sloppy, and didn't enforce requirements; because state charter offices were often badly understaffed; and because the real purpose of some charters was to grease the skids for vouchers. When charters shut down, typically it's because they've cooked the books or engaged in actual criminal activity, not because they've failed the children.

An analysis of NAEP data from 2003 found charters scoring lower than public schools, even when schools were matched for socioeconomic status and ethnic mix (National Center for Education Statistics, 2004). This report drove charter backers nuts. The reaction and sound refutation of that reaction appeared as *The Charter School Dust-Up* (Carnoy, Jacobson, Mishel, & Rothstein, 2005). Data from the 2007 NAEP assessment report indicate charters score lower than regular public schools, but at a more refined level, the data look mixed: Black urban kids in charters scored lower than their peers in regular public schools, but Hispanics did about as well. In any case, charters are a long way from the stellar examples that advocates such as Nathan expected them to be (Robelen, 2008).

Former Assistant Secretary of Education, Chester E. Finn, Jr., voiced a reaction common to charter school advocates: "I'm not very interested in the average performance of charters. The word 'charter' signals so little about them, and the diversity within that universe is at least as great as the diversity outside it" (Robelen, 2008). Try substituting "public school" for "charters" in the preceding statement. Yet Finn and similar critics have for years had no trouble bashing the average public school and ignoring the "diversity within that universe."

As for vouchers, Reagan had proposed vouchers using taxpayer money to allow students to attend private schools. He had little success. He was preceded by Richard Nixon who had actually taken the idea from Lyndon Johnson (the idea of vouchers was not always in the conservative domain). Everyone, it seems, wanted vouchers—except the people. Referenda in many states lost by big margins, even when advocates outspent opponents, as was true in California and Michigan in 1996 (a common cry after a defeat has been that the measure was ahead in the polls, causing the anti-voucher National Education Association to pour in huge sums of money to doom the referendum).

Finally, Milwaukee, urged by state legislator Polly Williams and assisted by a million-dollar public relations budget from the conservative Bradley Foundation, pushed through a limited voucher law, limiting enrollment to 1% of the student population and excluding religious schools (a provision later ruled unconstitutional by the Wisconsin Supreme Court; currently, up to 15,000 of the students are eligible) (Clowes, 2000).

The promise of voucher advocates was three-fold: Children using them could escape failing schools, their achievement would rise, and the failing public schools would improve because of the competition. How would we know? Test scores, of course. When the test scores failed to show any improvement, no matter how they were statistically tortured or processed through statistical procedures that made unrealistic assumptions, parental satisfaction became the primary reason for carrying on with vouchers. One study did find an improvement in math, but not in reading, in the Milwaukee program. The researcher, though, also noticed that the voucher kids were in small classes, and when she compared them with demographically matched public school students, the voucher advantage in math disappeared (Rouse, 2000).

In the middle of 2008, a report appeared claiming that, in the previous school year, students attending voucher schools had graduated at a much higher rate than those attending public schools (86% vs. 58%) (Warren, 2008). This difference seems improbable to me: in the previous 3 years the differences had been much smaller and, in 1 of the 3, Milwaukee public schools had graduated students at a higher rate. A voucher advocacy group sponsored the study and the report never named the schools involved. *Milwaukee Journal Sentinel* education reporter Alan Borsuk advised that he thought the bulk of the high schools were likely to be the old, established schools of Milwaukee, not any that had sprung up to feed off of vouchers (Borsuk, personal communication, June 2, 2008).

The laments of those who are hypercritical of public schools invariably involve test scores. Here's the test-score headline you never read: "AMERICA HAS BY FAR THE LARGEST NUMBER OF STUDENTS IN THE HIGHEST-SCORING GROUP IN PISA." It is, nevertheless, true (Salzman & Lowell, 2008). No one else even comes close. For the U.S., the figure is about 67,000 students. For second-place Japan, it is about 34,000. For third-place U.K., it is about 20,000. For top-ranked Finland, it is about 2,000. The 2,000 represents about 3.9% of Finnish students who took PISA, a second-place position after New Zealand with 4% (Salzman & Lowell, 2008).

The media and school critics really got out the long knives when the "final year of secondary school"[8] results of the Trends in International Mathematics and Science Study (TIMSS) were released and it appeared that American students had done very poorly. Appeared might well be the operative word (this and all of the international studies to be mentioned here are discussed in more detail in chapter 3). The eighth-grade results had been average and were called "mediocre," while the fourth-grade results were good and had been ignored, although Bennett would combine the three results and state in a speech to the Heritage Foundation, "In America today the longer you stay in school, the dumber you get relative to your peers in other industrialized nations." It became a popular refrain among school bashers (the talk is no longer available on the Heritage Foundation Web site) (Bennett, 2001).

---

8   It was called the "Final Year" of secondary school study because the authors were acutely aware that that final year represented vastly different experiences in different countries. The U.S. Department of Education and the U.S. media showed no respect for these differences and assumed a senior-is-a-senior-is-a-senior.

In addition to four administrations of TIMSS, we have had two rounds of Program of International Student Assessment (PISA), which tests 15-year-olds in reading, math, and science for the Organisation for Economic Co-operation and Development.

The results from the first PISA arrived on Pearl Harbor Day, December 7, 2004.[9] Here's a sampling of headlines: "Economic Time Bomb" (*The Wall Street Journal*), "Math + Test = Trouble for the U.S. Economy" (*The Christian Science Monitor),* "In a Global Test of Math Skills, U. S. Students Behind the Curve" (*The Washington Post),* "Math and Science Tests Find 4th and 8th Graders in U.S. Still Lag" (*The New York Times).*

The newspapers soon had lots of company. Writing in *Education Week,* Anthony Carnevale of the Center on Education and the Economy said, "Are international results a cause for concern? You bet. You don't have to have the math scores of a rocket scientist to know that in the new high-tech economic world, math and science is [*sic*] a key asset to global competition" (Carnevale, 2005) In the same issue, Hoover Institute's Eric Hanushek offered, "The fact is that these [international] results signify something real. Think of these assessments as early-warning signals for later economic welfare" (Hanushek, 2005). To the best of my knowledge, Hanushek has not related in any public forum the current global economic debacle to test scores.

Kurt Landgraf, CEO of ETS, chimed in with "According to ETS' most recent nationwide survey...76% of adults believe the U. S.

---

9   I should note that the years mentioned in this section are the years in which the reports were published. In chapter 3, they are discussed in terms of the years in which the data were collected, typically a year earlier.

will be less competitive 25 years from now if we don't fix our high schools today" (Educational Testing Service, 2005).

With PISA in mind, Bill Gates told the National Governors Association, "When I compare our high schools to what I see when I'm traveling, I am terrified for our workforce of tomorrow" (Pear, 2005).

This seems to be a very naïve view of what one sees in touring foreign schools. Years earlier, suspicious of the research of Harold Stevenson, I had asked Paul George, who had lived in Japan for a number of years and who had just written *The Japanese Secondary School* (which he considered horrible), how easy was it for international visitors to gain access to Japanese schools. He said, "Look, the high schools in Osaka are ranked 1 to 27 [from best to worst]. You can get into 1 and 2 easily. You might even get into 12 and 13. Not even Japanese researchers can get into 26 and 27." (George, 2000, personal communication). I imagine that's close to a cultural universal. People, and nations, want to show outsiders their best side.

By 2007, people who know nothing about tests were using them as policy devices. In early 2007, the U.S. Chamber of Commerce and the Center for American Progress (CAP) teamed up to produce a study, *Leaders and Laggards*. Can you imagine? Two organizations that ought to be perpetually at each other's throats teamed up to clobber schools. They painted the situation as grim:

> The measures of our educational shortcomings are stark indeed; most 4th and 8th graders are not proficient in reading or mathematics. Only about two-thirds of 9th graders graduate

from high schools within four years. And those students who do receive diplomas are too often unprepared for college or the modern workplace.

Despite such grim data, for too long the business community has been willing to leave education to the politicians and educators—standing aside and contenting itself with offers of money, support, and goodwill. (U.S. Chamber of Commerce, 2007)

On the contrary, the business community has been trying to control public education since at least the late 19th century. It wants schools to prepare students to work so it won't have to pay to train them. The business community makes no distinction between education and training.

When the report was rolled out for the press, John Podesta, former Clinton chief of staff, executive director of CAP, and recently co-chairman of President Obama's transition team, had this to say: "I find it *unconscionable* that there is not a single state in the country where a majority of 4th and 8th graders are proficient in math and reading" (Podesta, 2007).

While Podesta was finding this situation unconscionable, Richard Rothstein and his colleagues at Columbia University were releasing a study showing that *there is no country in the world that has a majority of its students proficient in reading* (Rothstein, Jacobsen, & Wilder, 2006). And, at the American Institutes for Research, former acting commissioner of the National Center for Education Statistics, Gary Phillips, was releasing a more extensive study finding that *only five nations have a majority proficient in math* (Singapore, 75%; Korea, 65%; Hong Kong, 64%; Japan, 61%; and

Taiwan, 61%). In reading, no country *comes close* to having a majority proficient. Sweden is tops with 33% (U.S. about 31%; Finland did not take part in this particular study). A mere two nations had a majority of their students proficient in science (Taiwan, 51%; Singapore, 51%) (Phillips, 2007).

What Rothstein and Phillips had done was build on a technique first developed by Robert Linn, a much honored psychometrician at the University of Colorado. The logic of the technique is simple. We know how American students do on both NAEP and international tests. We know how students in other countries do on international tests. That makes it possible to estimate how they would do were they to sit down for our NAEP assessments.

Of course, the ringer in all of this discussion is the word *proficient*, which is misunderstood by many. "Proficient" is a common word so we assume we know what it means, but we don't. We can point to the proficient level on NAEP tests, which is what most people have in mind when they use the word. But the NAEP achievement levels, as we shall see in chapter 3, are essentially meaningless and set at a totally unrealistic level. They were *designed* by Chester Finn, at the time president of the National Assessment Governing Board, to sustain the sense of crisis established first by *Sputnik* and more recently by *ANAR*.

Eli Broad and Bill Gates spent $50 million to establish Ed in '08 to make education a big issue in the 2008 presidential campaign. However, a former Clinton official told me, on condition of anonymity, he had advised both Senator Clinton and Senator Obama not to say *anything* about education, because anything about education would make *somebody* mad. Except in their speeches to the National Education Association, they dutifully took the advice.

The hammer that drove education into the ground as an issue, of course, was the economy. At first the problem seemed limited to the U.S. and to the problems created by subprime mortgages. But then it swept across the world. Iceland—Iceland!—became a basket case. The cover of the April 2009 *Vanity Fair* reads, "How Iceland Went Pfft," noting in the article that Iceland's debt is 850% of its GDP (Lewis, 2009). National banks, including ours, poured huge sums into the system to shore it up. But banks and other institutions refused to loan—they had money, but the credit system froze up.

Naturally, when TV's talking heads discuss the current state of affairs as the worst thing since the 1980s recession and maybe the worst since the Great Depression and people are watching their 401(k)s move towards 000(k)s, education reform suddenly looks like a trivial exercise.

To the best of my knowledge, no one has said a single word about this debacle being the fault of the schools. And a good thing, too. Japan's kids score well on tests but, in 2008, Japan's economy, the second largest in the world, shrank three times as much as the U.S. economy (McCurry, 2009).

If it is the fault of any schools, it is the fault of the business schools who failed to instill an appropriate sense of ethics and appreciation of risk in their graduates. That the schools have escaped blame (so far) might be a first in the history of finding scapegoats for social crises.

In fact, the situation leads me to say something I'm sure educators and their critics alike will not be happy to hear: compared to the mammoth tsunami unleashed by bad economic and investing decisions, school effects are like a wave caused by dropping a pebble in a pond.

Still, some $100 billion of the Obama administration's recovery plan goes to public school and colleges over a 2-year period. Secretary of Education Arne Duncan has great discretion in how to spend some $54 billion intended to prevent layoffs (Dillon, 2009). Duncan has been relatively vague about plans (not surprising; as of this writing he has only had the money for 2 weeks), but some of the notions put forward leave one scratching one's head. At a time when districts are considering moving to a 4-day week to save money, Duncan has proposed a longer school year. He wants to spend even more money on testing.

Duncan has used the "C" word: crisis. "We're not just facing an economic crisis here in America. I'm absolutely convinced we are facing an education crisis as well" (Hernandez, 2009). His comments indicated little sense of the "crises" we faced in education in 1957 (*Sputnik*), 1967 (ghetto riots), 1977 (*On Further Examination*), 1983 (*A Nation at Risk*), 1998 (international test score comparisons), and 2002 (NCLB).

Rise of Standardized Tests

Now, back to the topic at hand, a short history of the rise of the almighty standardized test. Those who have tried to counter the misinformation about tests, especially about tests and competitiveness, have been few, and their efforts have often been ignored or worse. After *Washington Post* columnist Richard Cohen wrote "Johnny's Miserable SAT's" in 1990, I fired back with "SAT Scores: Miserable or Miraculous?" (Bracey, 1990). The group that established an average score of 500 on the SAT were 10,654 kids mostly in the northeast. Ninety-eight percent were White, 61% male, and 41% had attended private, college preparatory high schools (Angoff, 1971). By 1990, 52% of the seniors were girls, 29% were minorities, and 87% attended public institutions. Many more in 1990 came from low-income families than in the 1941 elite (College Board, 1990). Taking all that change into account, the scores did indeed tend toward the miraculous side.

Iris Rotberg, then at the National Science Foundation, Harold "Bud" Hodgkinson, Richard Jaeger of the University of North Carolina at Greensboro, and Harold "Doc" Howe of Harvard, wrote pieces favorable to schools. Nobody paid much attention. My article got the eye of a group of engineers at Sandia National Laboratories in Albuquerque, authors of "The Sandia Report" mentioned earlier (Carson, Huelskamp, & Woodall, 1993). As I understood the story, Secretary of Energy Watkins announced in a speech that education would be a priority at Sandia (the Department of Energy funds Sandia National Labratories).

My sense is that the engineers got wide-eyed and they looked at each other with a "Wha?" expression. But, being engineers, they figured they'd better look at the system which had been given a priority status. They found some good things and some bad things, but the closing sentence of the draft edition said "There are many serious problems in the American education but there is no system-wide crisis."

One of them visited me in Colorado, and after his presentation, I suggested that we put all the data together and publish somewhere. He said something like "We can't. We've got internal political problems." And he recalled going to Washington, DC, to present the findings to congressional staffers and members of the Departments of Energy and Education. The Sandia engineer told me that then-Deputy Secretary of Education, David Kearns had said, "You bury this, or I'll bury you" (personal communication). An *Education Week* story about the suppression of the report said "Administration officials, particularly Mr. Kearns, reacted angrily at the meeting" (Miller, J., 1991).

The Sandia engineer said, though, that they didn't need to see their names on an essay and urged me to publish on my own and, after failing to place it in popular press outlets, I sent it to *Phi Delta Kappan* as "Why Can't They Be Like We Were?" The title is a snippet of a lyric from a 1960 musical, *Bye Bye Birdie:* "Why can't they be like we were, perfect in every way? Oh, what's the matter with kids today?" (Bracey, 1991). The Sandia Report eventually appeared as the entirety of the May/June edition of the *Journal of Educational Research* where it was seen by, maybe, 5,000 people, no journalists among them (Carson et al., 1993).

David Berliner and Bruce Biddle wrote *The Manufactured Crisis*, which contained not only the data I had used for my piece, but even more data and a long section identifying *real* education problems and possible ways to ameliorate them (Berliner & Biddle, 1995). Colleagues asked Berliner if he then felt marginalized. He said no, but many professors at large research universities are deeply invested in perceived school failures, using them to liberate money from governments and foundations ("Here's this terrible problem in education; give us some money and we'll try to fix it"). I think it is telling that, in the 18 years since my first article appeared (first, because it became an annual report appearing each October in *Phi Delta Kappan*), I have been invited to speak at only one large research university, Indiana University in Bloomington. I have had many invitations from smaller universities that have large undergraduate teacher preparation programs (Indiana University has that, too, and, as a possible additional factor, I used to teach there).

When Bruce Smith retired as editor of *Phi Delta Kappan* in 2008, one of the reasons he gave me was that each day he felt more and more like Sisyphus. It would be one thing if there were something new and something constructive, but how many times can the PISA math and science rankings be rolled out, while ignoring TIMSS and PIRLS and employers' cries for employees with "soft skills" that are not obtained from tests?

Chris Gallagher, at the University of Nebraska at Lincoln, worked closely with the Nebraska Department of Education as they developed assessments engaging both students and teachers. In the process, he evolved two "ideas," two contrasting models of school reform (in spite of the appalling overuse of the word, one is tempted to call them "paradigms" because the differences between them are so large). (See Figure 2.1)

I would tweak only one thing—the accountability model's "assessment of learning" is usually *not* of learning. It's a measure of achievement confounded with family and community models. The growth models do a better job of assessing actual learning.

A new model that assesses "impact" growth of learning in school vs. growth of learning in time outside of school has at least the potential to do better yet (Downey, von Hippel, & Hughes, 2008). Gallagher's model as applied specifically to testing is provided at the end of chapter 3.

Figure 2.1. Contrasting Models of School Reform	
Accountability	Engagement
Business model	Democratic model
School reform	School improvement
Teachers as impediments to reform	Teachers as leaders of school improvement
One-way relationships	Mutual relationships
Student achievement	Student learning
Test based	Assessment informed
Standardization	Standards
Stern-father morality	Shared-responsibility ethic
Transaction	Interaction
Top-down	Bottom-up (or inside out)
Exerts control	Builds capacity
High stakes	High impact
Unearned distrust	Earned trust
Competition	Collaboration
Compliance	Commitment
Assessment *of* learning	Assessment *for* learning
Demands simplicity	Embraces complexity

Source: Gallagher, 2007, p. 29

Chapter 3:
Tests: Descriptions and Trends—
How Do We Measure Up?

Evaluating schools with standardized test scores is like evaluating prospective defensive football tackles only on how fast they can run the 40-yard dash. Actually, it's closer to evaluating them on how fast they can run the 100-yard dash. That's something they will never have to do in a real game and thus is not a valid measure of how well they can play the game. Once people leave educational institutions, they don't usually have to take any test that looks like what they suffered through in school.

In the case of defensive tackles, even the 40-yard dash is not a particularly important indicator—they're not going to run fast enough to catch a running back or an wide end, although they might move fast enough for 10 yards or so to cut off a running back.

But schools, teachers, principals, districts, states, and nations *are* evaluated by tests. Worse, people make false assumptions about tests (e.g., that they are linked in some meaningful way to the nation's economic competitiveness). They believe that test scores are falling (they are not) and that American kids are falling ever farther below other nations (not true, and on one set of tests, American kids showed more growth over an 8-year period than all but 3 of the nations involved, Latvia, Lithuania, and Hong Kong) (Mullis, Martin, Gonzalez, & Chrostowski, 2004, pp. 42-43).

So, let's take a quick review of the tests that are out there and of score trends on those tests. Nationally, we have the SAT, the ACT, the National Assessment of Educational Progress (NAEP), and a few states still administer a nationally normed norm-referenced test. Finally, each state has a "criterion-referenced test" (we will learn why those quote marks are there later). Internationally, we have TIMSS, PISA, and PIRLS. Evaluating the unique state-developed tests used to measure state standards, and usually used to comply with NCLB requirements as well, is beyond the scope of this book.

The SAT (Scholastic Aptitude Test)

The College Entrance Examination Board (now simply College Board) was formed in 1900, and mostly consisted of Ivy League, Seven Sisters, and a few other Northeastern colleges. The south-ernmost school was Johns Hopkins in Baltimore. The schools wanted both to bring some coherence to high school curricula and to predict who would succeed at institutions of higher education. The latter was rather a silly criterion since the high school gradu-ation rate was about 3% at the time, but the colleges had found that students whose course-taking records looked the same had, in fact, had vastly different experiences.

The Board began by giving essay examinations and grading them. The colleges objected to the latter practice, and the Board soon dropped it. Frederick J. Kelly, at the University of Kansas, invented the multiple choice question in 1915 (Hansen, 1993, p. 211). Kelly's innovation made it possible for the first time to give exactly the same test to masses of people simultaneously and not spend a fortune. This came in handy in World War I when the military wanted to sort masses of people and predict who would be good tank drivers or good pilots or who were ground soldiers.

The predictive power of the Army's tests impressed the Board. Its SAT began life in 1926 and contained both essay and multiple-choice questions. In 1941, World War II disrupted the calendar for the essays and the SAT became all multiple-choice. Its principal developer, Carl Campbell Brigham, displayed appropriate modesty about the capabilities of his child:

> The present state of all efforts of men to measure or in any way estimate the worth of other men, or to evaluate the results of their nurture, or to reckon their potential possibilities does not warranty any certainty of prediction. ...This additional test (the SAT) now made available through the instrumentality of the College Entrance Examination Board may help to resolve a few perplexing problems, but it should be regarded *merely as a supplementary record.* To place too great emphasis on test scores is as dangerous as the failure to properly evaluate any score or rank in conjunction with other measures and estimates which it supplements. (Brigham, 1926, in Angoff, 1971, emphasis added)

Would that the nation had heeded Brigham's warning!

The assumption underlying the SAT (and all standardized tests) was worthy but faulty: Giving exactly the same test under exactly the same conditions would make that test a "common yardstick," to use the oft-stated description. The Board was familiar with the curriculum in many high schools in the region, but out there in the hinterland was some brilliant young man at South Succotash High School who likely wouldn't come to the Board's attention. His only chance for an Ivy League education rested on his SAT scores.

At the time, most psychologists and psychometricians (testing folk) thought intelligence to be largely inherited and the SAT was sometimes referred to as an IQ test, even by ETS's first president, Henry Chauncey, although that notion later became anathema (Owen, 1985, p. 200). The idea that it was affected by parents and school quality was acknowledged (note the use of the word "nurture" in the quote from Brigham), but held to be quite weak compared to the forces of genes.

That a middle class or affluent student in, say, Princeton, New Jersey, would be much more likely to hear the word "regatta" and to know what it means than an impoverished rural or urban student didn't diminish the view that the SAT acted as a common yardstick, at least by the College Board, Ivy League Schools, and ETS (in chapter 7 we shall see that the nature-nurture controversy is based on a false, or, at least, obsolete, conceptualization).

In fact, during my years at ETS (1967-1970), an organizational spin-off from the Board and actual developer of the SAT, it was sacred that the SAT was impervious to coaching, to test preparation. When one of my colleagues committed the heresy of showing that coaching could influence both the verbal and mathematics portions, ETS fired him. Really.

We have already taken note of the SAT's much discussed decline starting in 1963. The mathematics score bottomed out in 1982 and then rose almost constantly, reaching a high of 520 in 2005 before dipping 2 points in 2006 and 1 point in 2007. The path of the SAT verbal has not been so consistent. The verbal score dropped in 1983 at 503 and rose to a high of 508 in 2004 and 2005, but then dipped and now stands at 502.

All of the above scores come from the "recentered" scale the Board created in 1995. The "recentered" scale is nothing more than a renormed scale, something that occurs all the time to norm-referenced tests. Viewed from one perspective, the SAT is a norm-referenced test. In 1941, the average raw score converted to a scaled score of 500, and the standard deviation, a measure of how much the scores vary from the average, was set to 100. All scores were then referenced to the "norm" of 500. These are straightfor-ward statistical procedures.[10]

The SAT never represented the scores of the typical student ap-plying to college. As noted on page 68, the norms originally were set on a group of 10,654 seniors mostly living in New England and New York. Ninety-eight percent were White; 61% were male; and 41% had attended private, college-preparatory high schools (Angoff, 1971). In 1996 (the 1995 report is not on the Board's Web page, but 1996 would differ little), 1,153,755 students took the SAT, 58% were female, 71% were White, 25% came from homes with incomes under $30,000, and 83% attended public high schools (College Board, 1996). While the graduating class of 1941 did not represent the typical student applying to college, the class of 1996 also in no way represented the graduating class of 1941.

---

10   From another perspective, the SAT is a criterion-referenced test with the criterion being its ability to predict success in college.

Perhaps more importantly, if a student in 1995 learned that the average SAT total at a particular college was 1050 and hers or his was 1000, the student might well decide not to apply. This thinking ignores the variability around the average—some students will have scores higher than 1050 and some will have scores lower. It also implicitly and wrongly assumes that the SAT is *the* determinant of who gets into where. This is not true. For instance, Brown University could fill *two* freshmen classes just with students who score 750-800 on the SAT verbal, but, in fact, admitted only about one-third of these applicants and admitted a number with scores in the 400s (Bracey, 1999).

The student seems more below average than is really the case because the student is being compared to the 1941 elite, not to the much larger group of students today. The recentering attempted to make the average of 500 actually represent the typical high school senior applying to college. But people went nuts about it, calling it an attempt to hide ignorance or to administer a big dose of educational Prozac.

The American College Test (ACT)

The ACT was developed to serve other regions of the nation and is the test of choice in most of the Midwestern and non-Atlantic southern states. The Pacific states tend to use both tests about equally. While the SAT focused on selecting the students most likely to succeed in elite colleges, the ACT has historically focused more on matching students to universities and on public institutions. Nicholas Lemann in his book, *The Big Test,* quotes from an ETS report that says, "ACT will deal with the great unwashed, the College Board will deal with the rest" (Lemann, 1999, p. 103). (Lemann's history of the College Board and ETS is a wonderful read, but his case for the SAT as a life-determining event in the second half of the book builds a theory that even he obviously doesn't believe.)

While the College Board has courted publicity—even created it—ACT has been more retiring. They have recently published reports claiming to analyze what percentage of students are "ready" for college. "Ready" in this instance is in terms of how likely the students are to pass certain courses. The students declared ready do indeed pass the courses at a higher rate than the unready, but substantial proportions of the unready also pass. To me, it does not look like a system that an *individual* can use well to determine where or whether he or she will go to college. I think Wilfrid Aikin's 1943 conclusion about the Eight-Year Study—that many roads lead to college success—still holds (the Eight-Year Study is discussed in chapter 10).

The National Assessment of Educational Progress (NAEP)

NAEP was the inspiration of Commissioner of Education Francis Keppel (the office did not reach Secretarial level until the Carter administration) in the mid-1960s. Ralph Tyler and psychometricians actually put it together. Keppel saw it akin to a health survey. You couldn't know how serious a tuberculosis situation might be until you knew how many people had contracted it. NAEP was to determine what people knew. Keppel didn't think they knew very much, but that was an empirical question, still.

Norm-referenced tests are composed of items that about 50% of the test takers get right. There are no really easy items and no really hard ones. NAEP, on the other hand, would ask some of those middle-difficulty items, but it would also ask questions it thought most people would get right (90%) and questions it thought few people (10%) would get right. For statistical reasons that needn't be explained here, this approach would prevent one from using NAEP results to make predictions about later behavior (as was done—as was the *purpose* of—the SAT and ACT). But that was okay. Keppel and Tyler saw NAEP as purely descriptive.

The professional education organizations opposed NAEP mightily, arguing that it would destroy local control, the keystone of our education system, would stamp out creativity and lead to cheating, and worst of all, would inevitably lead to a national curriculum under federal control (Hand, 1965). NAEP survived only when Keppel agreed to house it at the Education Commission of the States (ECS), which dealt with state policy issues, and to not report any scores at any smaller a level than "region"—northeast, south, etc. The regional reports were perfectly useless. For years, NAEP contracts were awarded to ECS on a noncompetitive basis, but as NAEP grew, and therefore became more lucrative for a contractor, pressure grew to have the NAEP contract go out on bid. When it did open up to bidding, ETS won and NAEP moved from ECS to ETS in 1983.

While the NAEP assessments were pretty good as tests go, they had at least one problem: they underestimated achievement because no one took them seriously. They blew into a child's life and out in one day, and neither the students, their parents, the teachers, or the administrators knew how well the students had done. I once mentioned this to Archie Lapointe, then NAEP's Executive Director. He laughed and said, yes, the biggest problem with NAEP was keeping the kids awake during the tests.

Its invisibility, while leading to underestimates of what people knew, was also a strength: it prevented NAEP from becoming a high-stakes test until after 1988. When a test attains high-stakes status, it unleashes many forces that corrupt it and diminish its validity (Nichols & Berliner, 2007). In 1988, the NAEP law was amended to permit state-by-state testing. That year Congress also established the National Assessment Governing Board to oversee policy issues. This led to a monumental change in NAEP that many of us see as negative. The National Assessment Governing Board established standards about what children *should* know. Before 1988, NAEP was purely descriptive; after 1988, it became prescriptive.

There are really two NAEPs. "Regular NAEP" tests reading and math and, less often, writing, civics, and science. The items in Regular NAEP change over time to accommodate changes in curriculum and the recommendations of subject area professionals. NAEP trends use the same items repeatedly.[11] The following show trends from NAEP's initiation to the most recently reported data, 2004 (National Center for Education Statistics, 2005).

---

11   Except for a dozen or so mathematics questions. The probabilities of getting these items right changed significantly when NAEP introduced a new, more modern, brand of calculator, an indication of how sensitive some items are to minor contextual changes.

Figure 3.1. Looking at Changes in NAEP Over Time: Simpson's Paradox at Work

When you compare groups over time, you have to either ensure that the groups keep the same composition or do something to take changes into account. NAEP reports typically do neither. That is unfortunate because American demographics are constantly shifting. For example, the eighth grade sample in the 2007 NAEP reading test contained 58% White students. In 1993, the figure was 73% (National Center for Education Statistics, 2008b).

The changing makeup of who takes the NAEP is important because Asian students (who make up a tiny proportion of the sample) and White students score higher than Black and Hispanic students. The scores of Black and Hispanic students are mostly improving, but as lower-scoring groups make up a larger and larger proportion of the total sample, their lower scores attenuate the overall average. An example will make this clear.

	Time 1	Time 2
	500	510
	500	510
	500	510
	500	510
	500	510
	500	510
	500	510
	500	430
	500	430
	400	430
Average	490	486

Let's say the 500s at Time 1 represent the SAT scores of White students and say the 400 represents the SAT scores of minority students at Time 1. The overall average score is 490 and the White-minority difference is 100 points. Time 2 is some time in the future and scores are scores of a different group of high school seniors, one with more minority students. Let the 510s represent the SAT scores of White students and the 430s the SAT scores of minorities.

Thus, we see that the scores of White students have risen—500 to 510. The scores of minority students have risen more—400 to 430. All groups show increases. The White-minority difference has fallen from 100 points to 80 points. Yet, the average score at Time 2 is *lower* than at Time 1, 486 vs. 490. Simpson's paradox strikes. The resolution of the paradox, of course, lies in the composition of the groups at the two different times. At Time 1, minorities constituted only 10% of the sample, but at Time 2, they made up 30% of the total group. Their scores, although rising, are still lower than White students and as they become a larger proportion of the total group, this has the effect of lowering the overall average.

This is no mere abstract matter. The College Board once decried that the SAT verbal scores had not changed from 1982 to 2002. But, when I analyzed them by ethnicity, I found gains for all ethnic groups, some of them quite large (Bracey, 2006b, p. 65). Again, the explanation for the difference in the whole-group trend and the trends for subgroups (ethnicities in this case) was explained by the changing composition of the whole sample. For example, in 1981, White students made up 85% of the SAT testees, but in 2005, only 63% (Bracey, 2006b, p. 64).

Test score *trends* for any test in the United States should be examined by ethnic group as well as by what the whole group shows.

NAEP Reading

If we look at NAEP reading trends for the nation, we see mostly three flat lines at all ages tested, 9, 13, and 17.

	1971	2004
9-year-olds	208	219
13-year-olds	255	259
17-year-olds	285	285

Most of the gain for the 9-year-olds occurred between 1999 and 2004. Then-Secretary of Education Spellings promptly credited NCLB, saying scores had risen more in that period than in the previous 28 combined. It was pointed out to Secretary Spellings that, given the haphazard, chaotic beginnings of NCLB in 2002-2003, most of the gain likely took place during the Clinton years. That did not change her rhetoric.

When one looks at reading scores by ethnicity, a different pattern emerges:

	1971	2004
White Students		
9-year-olds	214	226
13-year-olds	261	266
17-year-olds	291	293

For White students, gains appear only for the youngest students and do not show up later in assessments as these students move through school. (It should be noted, though, that the 13-year-olds are not the same students who were tested as 9-year-olds. The same is true for 17-year-olds.)

	1971	2004
Black Students		
9-year-olds	170	200
13-year-olds	222	244
17-year-olds	239	264

Black students show progress across all ages. The figures for 17-year-olds, though, are a bit misleading. Black 17-year-olds scored 243 in 1980, then peaked at 274 in 1988 and fell back to 261 in 1992. The decline alarmed many people and has never fully been explained. A recent book explores many possibilities, such as changing patterns of college attendance among parents, a growing income gap between Black and White parents, and trends in the racial composition of schools attended by Black students (Magnuson & Wolfogel, 2008). No definitive answers appear.

	1975	2004
Hispanic Students		
9-year-olds	183	205
13-year-olds	232	242
17-year-olds	252	264

Note that Hispanic students didn't form a sample large enough to be considered reliable until 1975, compared to 1971 for the other groups. Asian students have only recently become a large enough group to generate a reliable sample.

The trends for Hispanic students are not as smooth as for Black and White students. After rising steadily from 1975 to 1988, scores have bounced around continuously. Nine-year-old Hispanic students did show a sizeable gain from 193 to 205 (an all-time high) between 1999 and 2004. It will be interesting to see if the gain is maintained.

In any case, NAEP reading scores refute any contention that test scores are falling, a contention one often hears as if it is *such* a *known* fact that one need not verify it and one cannot challenge it. Well, as the 19th-century American humorist, Josh Billings, used to say, "It's better to know nothin' than to know what ain't so."

NAEP Mathematics

In mathematics, significant gains are seen in national data for all but 17-year-olds.

	1973	2004
9-year-olds	219	241
13-year-olds	266	281
17-year-olds	304	307

Again, the pattern is different when examined by ethnicity.

	1973	2004
White students		
9-year-olds	225	247
13-year-olds	274	288
17-year-olds	310	313

For White students, we see gains in 9-year-olds, which taper off and disappear by age 17.

	1973	2004
Black students		
9-year-olds	190	224
13-year-olds	228	262
17-year-olds	270	285

Black 9-year-olds register larger gains than White students and appear to be able to maintain some of that gain at later ages. The decline for 17-year-olds that appeared in the 1990s in reading is muted in math, as scores went from 289 in 1990 to 283 in 1999, rising back to 285 in the most recent assessment.

	1973	2004
Hispanic students		
9-year-olds	202	230
13-year-olds	239	265
17-year-olds	277	289

Like Black students, Hispanic students show large gains as 9-year-olds and hold on to some of it in later years.

NAEP trends in science have been discontinued. They showed patterns similar to mathematics up to 1999.

We should note that NAEP trends do not reflect the true growth of individuals. While the trend items remain constant, the students tested as 13-year-olds are not those who were tested as 9-year-olds, and those tested as 17-year-olds are not those who were tested at the two earlier ages.

People criticizing schools often use only the national averages, which they refer to as "stagnant." Of course, one should ask, "Given the attention to education reform after 1983, why do we not see more improvement?" One cannot answer that question, but one can argue that the descent into test mania that we have witnessed in this country is an ineffectual (at best) way to reform schools. In fact, the thesis of this book can be considered as showing that the test-and-punish approach to education reform simply does not work.

SAT Trends

We have discussed the SAT decline and its role leading us to a false and hysterical belief in tests. Here we take a more detailed look at trends. Using the recentered scale, College Board data show the SAT verbal hitting a low of 502 in 1981 and not moving much from that point since attaining a high of 509 in 1985 and 1986 and a new low of 499 in 1991 and 1994. The score for 2007 was 502.

The SAT math hit a low of 492 in 1980 and 1981, then rebounded to 520 in 2005. In the last 2 years, it has fallen to 518 (in 2006) and then 515 (in 2007) (College Board, 2008). The verbal has also declined. There is no clear reason why this should happen, although people speak of NCLB as polishing pebbles and dulling diamonds: Its focus on raising everyone to a minimally acceptable level may be having deleterious effects on able students, although one study failed to find evidence of a "Robin Hood" effect using NAEP data (Duffett, Farkas, & Loveless, 2008). At least one study reported that teachers were to ignore the "sure things" and "hopeless cases" in preparing students for an NCLB test, and to focus on those who might, with additional attention, pass the test (Booher-Jennings, 2005).

An email in June from a teacher said, not for attribution, her school referred to them as "tippers," as in "tipping point." With extra help, they might tip the school into a position of making AYP. The administration advises not to use any "demeaning" language about why these kids are being yanked from their regular classes. But these kids get the picture; they know why they're being taken out—and they feel awful; "like blockheads," said the teacher.

In addition, Robin Hood can steal a lot more than just test scores. Susan Goodkin and David Gold saw it this way:

> No Child is particularly destructive to bright young math students. Faced with a mandate to bring every last student to proficiency, schools emphasize incessant drilling of rudimentary facts and teach that there is one "right" way to solve even higher order problems. Yet one of the clearest indicators of a nimble math mind is the ability to see novel approaches and shortcuts to attacking such problems. Creativity is what makes math fun for those students....

> Talented writers fare no better in language arts education. Recently, a noted children's author recounted her dismay when fifth-graders attending one of her workshops balked at a creative writing exercise. She was shocked to learn that the reluctant learners were gifted. The children, however, had spent years completing mundane worksheets designed for struggling classmates and thus rebelled at an exercise they assumed would be another tedious worksheet. (2007, p. 13)

International Comparisons

International comparisons began in the 1960s. The first ones suffered severe methodological problems, particular the attempt to get a representative sample from all countries. The comparisons talked about today are TIMMS and PISA. TIMSS tested 4th- and 8th-graders in 1995, 8th-graders in 1999, and 4th- and 8th-graders in 2003 and in 2008; 12th-graders were badly assessed in 1995 and another attempt was made in late 2008, with a report due in late 2009. PISA assessed 15-year-olds in reading, math, and science in 2003 and 2006. PIRLS assessed reading in 4th-graders in 2001 and 2006. TIMSS and PIRLS reports can be found at http://timss.bc.edu. The PISA results are at www.pisa.oecd.org. The perspective from the U.S. Department of Education on all three programs can be found at www.nces.ed.gov.

As noted, the critics have come to all but ignore TIMSS, citing only the ranks on PISA. This is unfortunate not only because the U.S. shows better on TIMSS and PIRLS, but, as we shall see shortly, PISA has many deficiencies.

The original administration of TIMSS in 1995 also provides interesting information on how school critics operate. The first data to be released were the 8th-grade results from the 41 nations participating at that level. American students got 53% of the items correct, while the international average was 55%. In science, American 8th-graders got 58% correct, while the international average was 56%. Average performances in both cases, but only *The New York Times* and *Education Week* actually used the word "average." Many other media outlets used the term "mediocre." But average is a statistic, mediocre is a judgment (Beaton, Mullis, Martin, Gonzalez, Kelly, & Smith, 1996a, 1996b).

At the 4th-grade level, American students ranked 9th of 26 in math, and 3rd in the world in science. These results got very little media attention.

What did get a lot of attention were the results from the study of the "Final Year of Secondary School." This was a carefully chosen title because the directors of the study knew well that, after eighth grade, many differences appeared in nations in terms of the programs provided. Most American students attend a comprehensive high school (albeit, there can be substantial tracking within that school). Many countries have differentiated curricula that send students to different schools. While countries had been required to use representative samples of all students in a grade at grades 4 and 8, they were allowed to choose whom to test in the final year in the topics of physics and advanced mathematics. Many of the tested students were older than American students, although a few were younger. The directors of the study were nervous about cross-national comparisons based on simple ranks.

Not so for the American administrators and the American media. The scenario quickly degenerated to this: our seniors went up against their seniors and got stomped; our best and brightest seniors went up against their best and brightest seniors and got stomped. (For more of my thoughts on this topic refer to the May 2000 issue of *Educational Researcher*, Bracey, 2000b.)

TIMSS also led to one of the most often spouted clichés in education: The U.S. mathematics curriculum is a mile wide and an inch deep. But a study linking TIMSS and NAEP indicated that a number of U.S. states were outscored by only a few countries in math and only one in science. Similarly, breakouts by ethnicity shows some American groups doing well and others poorly.

Here are three important points about U.S. performance on the TIMSS Final Year Study:

1. 55% of American students worked at a paid job more hours a week than the research says is good for school achievement (Mullis, Martin, Beaton, Gonzalez, Kelly, & Smith, 1998, p. 120).

2. The U.S. tested pre-calculus as well as calculus students. When I asked Larry Suter of the National Science Foundation why we had done that he said, "Just to see how they'd do." Well, they did awful. They scored 100 points lower than students who had actually taken calculus. The latter group was average among nations. I think it is fine to "see how they'd do." That can be useful information. But it should be explicitly and repeatedly explained to the media and the public (Suter, 1998, personal communication).

3. I have made only informal inquiries about the existence of "senioritis" or the "senior slump" in other nations. Most respondents have said "not likely" because students are preparing for important—sometimes life-determining—college entrance tests. We tested American seniors in May (Mullis et al., 1998, p. 14). In May!

A YouTube segment from www.GOODmagazine, sponsored by ED in '08, "The State of American School" (www.youtube.com/watch?v=kLBZqrzZvk8), shows pictures of people graduating and says that as recently as 40 years ago the U.S. had the highest high school graduation rate, now we're 19th. The clip then asks "What Happened?" A screen with a bar graph appears; one bar, in pink, shows American scores and others, in black, depict other nations. The caption reads that the math and science scores of American 4th-graders stayed the same and others got better. The black bars grow in height, surpassing the American level. How's that for a *non-sequitur*, linking graduation rates to the ability of 4th-graders to bubble in answer sheets? It's also not true and one can also wonder, since 8th-graders took part in this study, why the 8th-grade scores are not also used. It's the same reason that *ANAR* used only one NAEP trend line—the data don't help the fearmongers make their case.

The true case: American 4th-grade TIMSS scores declined 5 points in science and 0 points in math. But, the other 14 countries in the study do not, by and large, rush past them. In math, 3 of the 14 countries lost ground and only 7 of the 14 scored higher than the U.S. The other 7 were lower in 1995 and lower in 2003. In science, 4 nations lost ground between 1995 and 2003—Japan, Netherlands, Australia, and Scotland. Only four nations scored higher than the U.S. in 2003, and of those, two—Scotland and Hong Kong—had scored lower in 1995. The other 10 nations scored lower in both 1995 and 2003 (Mullis et al., 2004).

The fourth round of TIMSS arrived in early December, 2008. It showed gains in mathematics for American students in both grades. Fourth-graders scored 529 compared to 518 in 1995. American 8th-graders went from 492 to 508 in the same period, but were at 502 in 1999 and 502 in 2003, so the gains in the past 4 years are minimal. In terms of rankings, of the 35 other nations participating at the 4th-grade level, 8 outscored the U.S., 4 had similar scores, and 23 scored lower. At the 8th-grade level, among the other 47 countries taking part, 5 had higher scores, 5 had similar scores, and 37 had significantly lower scores (Mullis, Martin, & Foy, 2008).

That there are not many countries scoring ahead of the U.S. is more cheering than that so many countries score lower. As TIMSS has expanded from its initial round in 1995, it has had few places to look except in the third world and such countries (to name only a few) as Kuwait, Botswana, and Algeria score low. At the 4th-grade level, Yemen set an all-time TIMSS low at 224 (the international average is 500 and most developed nations score between about 475 and 600) (Mullis et al., 2008).

National Public Radio reported that the good news was that American kids had gained, but the bad news was that other nations had gained more. This is not strictly true. Among the leading 5 nations at grade 8 mathematics, Singapore, Hong Kong (from 569 to 572), and Japan all scored substantially lower than in 1995. Only Taiwan and Korea showed gains.

In 4th-grade science, 4 nations scored higher, 6 scored about the same, and the rest scored lower. At the 8th-grade level, 9 scored higher, 3 scored the same, and the remainder scored lower. Yemen "bested" its math score, coming in at 197. U.S. science scores have not moved much since the program began in 1995—we looked good then, we look good now. But American media are good at ignoring looking good. *The Washington Post's* lead paragraph was,

> U.S. students are doing no better on an international science exam than they were a decade ago, a plateau in performance that leaves educators and policymakers worried about how schools are preparing students to compete in an increasingly global economy. (Glod, 2008)

Some media emphasized the gains in math (Dillon, 2008), some the "flatness" of the science scores, and George Miller (D-CA) commented fatuously: "It's increasingly clear that building a world class education system that provides students with a strong foundation in math and science must be part of any meaningful long-term recovery strategy" (Toppo, 2008). However, there have been cycles of boom and bust that occur without influence from schools.

New York Times reporter, Sam Dillon managed to insert in his TIMSS article an editorial comment that reeks of a common sense that is all to uncommon when it comes to discussing these studies:

> Comparing educational performance in the United States, a diverse country of 300 million with 50 stated educational systems, with city-states like Singapore and Hong King, which have populations of 4.5 million and 6.9 million people, respectively, is a bit of apples and oranges. (Dillon, 2008)

In any case, there is nothing in the TIMSS data to suggest a deterioration in U.S. performance or a crisis in the school system.

Program of International Student Assessment (PISA)

The Program of International Student Assessment (PISA) is operated by the Paris-based Organisation for Economic Co-operation and Development (OECD). It tests 15-year-olds. That in itself is problematic because of 1) the different placements of 15-year-olds in different countries depending on when students start school, and 2) the different placement of 15-year-olds because of retention or acceleration. The basic findings can be located at NCES (National Center for Education Statistics, 2007b).

The big problem with PISA is trying to determine what it measures. While TIMSS has a few short-answer questions, it is by and large a multiple choice test with short stems that ask mostly about a single concept or topic. PISA has long, discursive questions, sometimes with irrelevant information. So whether the question is about math or science, it will have a heavy reading skills component and might also be testing the student's attention span and ability to separate wheat from chaff. These last two can be significant skills in themselves, but their presence only confounds things in PISA.

PISA officials claim that the items measure students' ability to apply skills to new settings and also measure material students might have learned out of school. These contentions are, to say the least, problematic. I don't think anyone has attempted any kind of construct validity study of PISA. See Figure 3.2 for a sample PISA math item and Figure 3.3 for a science item, with my annotations.

Figure 3.2. Sample PISA Math Item

Seal's Sleep

A seal has to breathe even when it is asleep in the water. Martin observed a seal for 1 hour. At the start of his observation, the seal was at the surface and took a breath. It then dove to the bottom of the sea and started to sleep. From the bottom it slowly floated to the surface in 8 minutes and took a breath again. In 3 minutes it was back at the bottom of the sea again. Martin noticed that this whole process was a very regular one.

After 1 hour the seal was a) at the bottom, b) on its way up, c) breathing d) on its way down.

Note: Obviously, to answer this question, test-takers have to play the "testing game." For instance, they must assume that "very regular" means that it always takes exactly 8 minutes to rise up, zero seconds to breathe, and exactly 3 minutes to dive. Given the speed of a seal in water, Martin couldn't possibly see to the depth it reached after a 3-minute descent. One wonders how well children who have never seen a seal would fare with this question.

Figure 3.3. Sample PISA Science Item

Chocolate Diet
A newspaper article recounted the story of a 22-year-old student named Jessica, who has a "chocolate diet." She claims to remain healthy, and at a steady weight of 50kg, whilst eating 90 bars of chocolate a week and cutting out all other food, apart from one "proper meal" every 5 days. A nutrition expert commented: I am surprised someone can live with a diet like this. Fats give her energy to live but she is not getting nearly enough vitamins. She could encounter serious health problems in later life.

In a book with nutritional values, the following data are applicable to the type of chocolate Jessica is eating all the time. Assume also that the bars of chocolate she eats have a weight of 100 grams.

Protein g	Fats g	Carbohydrates g	Minerals calcium iron	Vitamins A B C	Total Energy kJ
5	32	61	50 4	-- 0.20--	2142

The nutrition expert said that Jessica "...is not getting nearly enough vitamins." One of those vitamins missing in chocolate is vitamin C. Perhaps she could compensate for her shortage of vitamin C by including a food that contains a high percentage of vitamin C in her "proper meal every five days." Here is a list of types of food:

1. Fish   3. Rice
2. Fruit   4. Vegetables

Which two types of food from this list would you recommend to Jessica in order to give her a chance to compensate for her vitamin C shortage?

A. 1 and 2   D. 2 and 3
B. 1 and 3   E. 2 and 4
C. 1 and 4   F. 3 and 4

Note: Most of the information in this "item" is irrelevant to the problem (a second question does ask if all of the energy comes from fat). To get at the question's intent, which is "demonstrating knowledge and understanding of science in life and health," I would think the following stem would do as well: "The doctor tells you you aren't getting enough vitamin C and this might lead to health problems later on. Which two of the following foods might you increase to reduce or eliminate your vitamin C deficiency?"

One wonders how much students might be distracted thinking about the quirkiness of a girl who eats almost 20 pounds (19.84) of chocolate a week (the story is real, taken from a newspaper account).

In the U.S., PISA has been generally accepted. According to some European acquaintances, I seem to be the only American with a problem about it. Not so with Europeans. I think this is because critics here use PISA just as a general cudgel: We rank low so we have to get on the stick and learn more math and science so we can produce more scientists and engineers and be competitive in the global economy. This is total nonsense, as we shall see in the next section, but PISA has not been used to make grand policy, curricular, and structural recommendations about American education.

Not so in Europe. While some European professors, especially in Francophone countries, have railed against the rankings as an "Anglo-Saxon model" to the detriment of broad and long-term effects, others have taken it as an indictment of the system. Nowhere was this more true than in Germany. When the first results were released in December 2001, *The Economist* ran the headline "Dummkopf!" Munich's *Suddeutsche Zeitung* had it as "PISA Debacle," while *Der Spiegel*, a German *Time*, asked "Are German Students Stupid?" *Frankfurter Allgemeine Zeitung's* headline was a demand: "Fix Our Schools."

Now a group of Austrian, Danish, French, German, English, and Norwegian researchers have struck back with an awkwardly titled book, *PISA According to Pisa* (*PISA zufolge PISA*) (Hopmann, Brinek, & Retzl, 2008). I say awkward because the book's 16 chapters critique PISA, some of them damningly so.

I am not alone in wondering what PISA measures. The math test correlates with the reading test +.77, meaning there is a great deal of overlap. Some items are multiple choice, but some call for an extended response, and these are often long, discursive, and contain irrelevant and/or factually wrong material. And, one must wonder about the fidelity of the translations for more than 50 nations. The OECD, PISA's sponsor, has been secretive about releasing items for public scrutiny. Perhaps with good reason. One released item is "A Copying Machine for Living Beings," a story about cloning. In his chapter in the book, Svein Sjøberg of the University of Oslo observes that the headline of the article was translated word for word into Norwegian, rendering it meaningless.

PISA items are supposed to begin life as "authentic text," meaning it was published somewhere. Professional item writers revise the text, and consensus must occur among all countries that the item is culturally neutral. At least, that's the official story.

In fact, the European investigators found instances of cultural bias. For instance, one reading item was based on an Algerian folk tale about a king who disguises himself in order to watch a reputedly wise judge without the judge knowing of the king's presence. In one of the cases in the story, two men, a peasant and a scholar, each claim the same woman is his wife. The judge tells them to leave her with him and return the next day. When they come back, the judge awards the woman to the scholar. He had called her into his quarters and asked her to refill his inkwell which she "cleaned quickly and deftly and filled with ink; therefore it was work she was accustomed to." The wife of a peasant would not know how to perform this task, so she must be the scholar's wife (PISA, 2006).

If PISA officials are secretive about releasing items, they are even more so about releasing the answers given by students in the extended response sections of the test. Seeing extended answers could provide insights about students' thinking. So far, only Luxembourg has published the answers students gave, and in some instances it is clear that the students did not understand what the item writers were trying to ask.

No uniform rules exist for who may be excused from testing, and different countries use different criteria. Stories persist about certain pupils being told to stay home on testing day (for example, Wuttke, 2007, personal communication). Sjøberg says most students in Scandinavia have never seen a test like PISA and don't take it seriously. On the other hand, in Taiwan, observers reported that parents gathered with their students on the grounds of the school and exhorted them to do well; the students marched into school to the national hymn and heard another exhortatory speech from the principal before taking the test (Sjøberg, in Hopmann et al., 2008).

In Singapore, as the test approaches, special cases are put up in stores, the lower level containing painkillers, presumably for headaches induced by studying for the test. No mention is made of the function of these painkillers besides reducing pain, but some versions of the medication shown in a picture in the book do contain caffeine, so it is possible that the pills are being hawked as performance enhancers. The upper shelf contains test-prep booklets (whose effectiveness is unknown) (Sjøberg, in Hopmann et al., 2008).

We tend to think of students as students as students, but, when it comes to test taking, this is not true. Dutch students try to answer all questions, which causes many of them to run out of time and having to guess. Austrian and German students skip many items and so do not face this problem. Greek students seem unaware of the time limits. They start off well, but get few items right near the end. In some countries, students are unfamiliar with the American-style one-right-answer multiple-choice questions and check multiple answers. Of course, it takes longer to try to figure out if more than one answer could be correct than to seek a single right answer (Wuttke, in Hopmann et al., 2008).

There are technical glitches in PISA beyond this small review, but some of the chapter titles are themselves revealing: "Disappearing Students: PISA and Students with Disabilities"; "Uncertainties and Bias in PISA"; "England: Poor Survey Response" (so many schools declined to participate that meaningful data could not be generated); "PISA and 'Real Life Challenges': Mission Impossible?" and "PISA—Undressing the Truth or Dressing up a Will to Govern?" Several authors point out that OECD is an organization that would push math and science and free market economics, but would not be interested in solidarity with the poor or working on sustainable development.

Progress in International Reading Literacy Study (PIRILS)

No matter what one might think about E. D. Hirsch, Jr.'s contentions overall, when he asserts that you test better on topics you are familiar with, he is irrefutably correct. American kids mostly do not know the metric system. The math and science questions were written only in metric.

In reading, the U.S. scored 542 in 2001 and 540 in 2006, both scores being well above the international average of 500. In the first instance, among 35 education systems, 3 were significantly higher, 9 were not significantly different from the U.S., and 23 were significantly below (this is a statistical test of significance; it is not necessarily related to any kind of practical significance). In 2006, among 45 participating systems, 38 of which were nations, 10 scored higher, 13 the same, and 22 lower (Elley, 2002; Mullis, Martin, Kennedy, & Foy, 2007; National Center for Education Statistics, 2007a). Not a bad outcome. But tongues clucked and then-Secretary of Education Spellings had a typical, if irrelevant, reaction: "Clearly, as the world becomes flatter, it's becoming more competitive. We need to do better than simply keep pace." The article that quoted Spellings was itself headlined, "America Idles on International Reading Test" (Manzo, 2007). Why not "America Continues to Do Well on International Reading Test"?

It is probably cogent that all but two of the nations that scored higher tested older children than America. Luxembourg kids were more than a year older. The Russian Federation which gained 37 points from the 2001 administration garnered first place. *Education Week* reported that experts "were stunned by Russia's dominance" (Manzo, 2008). I'm not. I don't believe it.

The official story is that Russia added a year of education at the start of school between the 2001 and 2006 administrations. But Russian kids in the 2006 test were only 6 months older than those in 2001 (10.8 years vs. 10.3 years). I think something went awry in the sampling. The Russian 5th percentiles on the two assessments are similar, but the 95th percentiles differ by 60 points. That is an enormous change, a huge difference. Such a variation over 5 years challenges the credibility of the results.

I'm also wary of second-place Hong Kong, which jumped 36 points. It's been a long time since I lived in Hong Kong, but the principal mode of instruction, at least in public schools, was rote recital in unison of what the teacher said.

Only 10 of the 28 countries that participated in both assessments changed more than 10 points in either direction. If America "idles," virtually the whole world kept it in neutral, too. Kuwait did drop a whopping 66 points, which no one apparently noticed. Maybe that's because Kuwait doesn't even appear on the report's "Trends" page, but perhaps people only notice when countries make big gains relative to the U.S., not when they absorb big losses. When you see gains in a 5-year period like Russia's and Hong Kong's, and losses like Kuwait's, I believe you are safer to conclude that something went wrong with the testing procedures rather than that something changed in the educational system.

What's It All Mean?

So, after what has no doubt for many been a mind-numbing number of numbers, where are we?

We have seen that there are upward trends on the SAT and NAEP, gains in mathematics on TIMSS, and no hint of a decline anywhere. There is no "crisis."

And, while the achievement gap between Black students and Hispanic students on the one hand and White students on the other persists, there is nothing in the entire research literature to suggest a program like NCLB would reduce or eliminate that gap. NCLB simply says "do it." It provides no guidance, not even a hint of what states, districts, schools, or teachers can do to erase it.

It would be one thing if all of this testing could be linked to what happens later in life or the health of the economy, but it can't. No research shows anything other than test scores predict grades and other test scores. Limiting herself to international comparisons, Iris Rotberg wrote in *Education Week*, "The fact is that test-score comparisons tell us little about the quality of education in any country" (Rotberg, 2008). They don't predict life. Except indirectly (Baird, 1985; Munday & Davis, 1974). High test scores are not even what employers say they want. Test scores have never ranked high on employers' lists of desiderata and never less so than now, when employers say they want people who can work in diverse groups, who can see connections among fields, etc. (Barton, 2006; Handel 2005).

During the 1970s, many researchers explored the relationship between ability and achievement on the one hand and adult accomplishment on the other. "Adult accomplishment" was defined in a variety of ways, from income to productivity to awards in a field. The people at the American College Testing Program looked at the relationship between the ACT college admissions tests and accomplishment in leadership, music, literature, art, drama, and science, along with the college GPA (Munday & Davis, 1974).

The accomplishments ranged in stature from voting in a local, state, or national election, to actively campaigning for a candidate, to running for office. Each area had nine such indicators. The correlations for those who had not completed college were universally tiny, except for the composite score on the ACT with college GPA for women, .31. For graduates, the correlations were only slightly larger. The Composite ACT score with college GPA for men was .39. For women it was .29.

One can criticize this study for its timing—only 2 years after students who received a degree in 4 years would have graduated. But it seems to me that's the point. So many good things have happened to me by dumb luck or being in the right place at the right time that it would be hard to take credit for the outcomes that resulted or to assign them to academic talent. And, if I had been middle class or affluent or Black, everything might have turned out differently. In an exhaustive review, Baird concluded that high academic ability helps a student get more education, but it is the quality of the education that might be critical (Baird, 1985). One large study looked at how often 6,000 Ph.D.'s were cited in the Citation Index (a major statistic in the race towards promotion and tenure in higher education) and correlated that with ability measures. It was .04 for mathematics; .10 for physics; .07 for chemistry; .04 for biochemistry; and .07 for psychology. Virtually zero across the board (Baird, 1985).

Michael Petrilli of the Thomas B. Fordham Institute recently argued that the true genius of American education lies not in the classroom, but in the extensive program of extracurricular activities (Petrilli, 2008). He has no hard evidence for this, and nor do I, but I find the idea compelling. It is in the extracurricular activities that one develops and practices skills that will stand one in good stead in later years and on the job. They develop the personal qualities listed on page 4. One can even find a number of virtues learned in sports and activities that are often maligned as detracting from academics. Why do so many countries send people to U.S. schools? They want to figure out how to make their kids more creative, how to "produce the next Bill Gates or Sergey Brin, the next generation of innovators and entrepreneurs" (Petrilli, 2008). The mistake these visitors make though, says Petrilli, is that they look inside the classroom when they should be looking at the extracurricular activities outside of them. (Most countries, incidentally, do not have major sports teams attached to schools— they are attached to cities. Europeans are stunned at the palatial stadia and Olympic-sized swimming pools possessed by many U.S. high schools.)

In addition to extracurricular programs, most American students also work at a paying job some time during their high school career. As long as these jobs do not require more than 20 hours a week, they actually seem to improve school performance. They have also been cited as developing time management skills and a sense of responsibility to others who depend on the students to show up on time and get the job done. The insufferable "2 Million Minutes" shows American students working, with the clear implication that they ought to be "cooped up" as an Indian student puts it, and studying 24/7 (www.2millionminutes.com/index.asp). But the video really makes Petrilli's case that the genius of American education lies outside the classroom. The video follows two Americans, two Indians, and two Chinese students through their daily routines. The American boy works at a job, used to be the captain of the football team, and obtains a full scholarship to

Purdue in computer graphics. The American girl lands at Indiana University with a double major in Spanish and pre-med. The Indian and Chinese kids spend all their time studying and none of them get the colleges or programs they want. The video actually makes the point that the American students have options, the Indian and Chinese students do not.

I mentioned earlier that the U.S. produces the "lion's share" of high performers, as measured by international comparisons (Salzman & Lowell, 2008). The larger point is that comparing countries on *average* scores is a largely silly and irrelevant exercise. Salzman and Lowell argue that it is the top-performers that are likely to contribute to innovations in cutting-edge technology, not the average student. At the same time, they argue, low-performers might well act as a drag on the economy, and the downside of the international comparisons is that the U.S. contains more than its fair share of those, too.

Finally, it is important to note the position of British economist S. J. Prais. The fearmongers in this country take the test scores in international comparisons at face value and worry about our economic future. Prais looks at our economic performance and worries about the validity of the international comparisons: "That the U.S., the world's top economic performing country, was found to have schooling attainments that are only middling casts fundamental doubts about the value and approach of these [international] assessments" (Prais, 2008, p. 154). Salzman and Lowell would no doubt agree. My only objection to Prais's comment is that it is in reference to PISA, and, as shown above, it is doubtful that PISA measures "schooling attainments."

Chapter 4:
No Child Left Behind: "The Beatings Will Continue Until Morale Improves"

Nothing exemplifies the dark age of education, with which we are now hopefully done, better than No Child Left Behind.

I wrote my first anti-NCLB article for *Newsday* in 2001, a full year before what was then a nameless plan became law. I followed up with "NCLB: A Plan for the Destruction of American Public Education" (Bracey, 2002a), "The Perfect Law" (Bracey, 2004a), and "The Seven Deadly Absurdities of NCLB" (Bracey, 2004b). I am pleased to see that a wildly diverse group of people have now proposed educational reforms that would incorporate some of the "Seven Deadly" contentions (see www.boldapproach.org). This "Broader, Bolder Approach" realizes that schools cannot do it all by themselves. President Obama has also proposed "Promise Neighborhoods" that would incorporate the work of a number of early-childhood advocates, especially that of Geoffrey Canada and his "Harlem Children's Zone" (Tough, 2008). See Figure 4.1 for a brief review of those absurdities, so visible from the start.

Figure 4.1. The Seven Deadly Absurdities of NCLB

1. NCLB uses the phrase "scientifically based research" 111 times in its 1,100 pages, but there is no research whatsoever that undergirds the law's approach to school reform. If anything, the research argues *against* NCLB.

2. Although some money comes with the program, NCLB relies almost solely on punishment. Most schools have to report test data for 37 subgroups. If any one subgroup fails to make AYP, the entire school is labeled a failing school. It is in the great tradition of "the beatings will continue until morale improves."

3. All students must be proficient in reading and mathematics by 2014. As numerous sane observers have pointed out, this is merely crazy as well as impossible (see, for example, Rothstein et al., 2006).

4. As a consequence of #3 above, California projects that, by 2014, 99% of its schools will be labeled as failing while in the six higher-scoring Great Lakes states, the failure rate will be a mere 95%, on average.

5. Schools that fail to make AYP for 2 consecutive years must offer all students the opportunity to leave the "failing" school, even if 36 of the 37 subgroups did make AYP. Groups most likely to not make AYP are special-needs students and English Language Learners (ELLs). Schools can also fail to make AYP if fewer than 95% of the students fail to show up on test day. If only 94% of the students take the test, the whole school fails.

6. NCLB depends solely on testing. Gone is any semblance of a *mens sana in corpore sano* (a sound mind in a sound body) view of education's goals. Even such initial NCLB stalwarts and educational conservatives as Chester Finn and Diane Ravitch have seen the craziness of this and have called for a liberal arts education for all children.

We should have seen this [obsession with test scores] coming. We and others who have pressed for higher academic standards in recent years—particularly since the Charlottesville education summit set national education goals in 1989—should have anticipated the "zero sum" problem that it would give rise to: more emphasis on some things would inevitably mean less attention to others. Insofar as we recognized this, however, we naïvely assumed that school days and years would expand to accommodate more of everything; that teachers would somehow become more knowledgeable; and that state and federal policy makers would insist on a balanced curriculum.

We were wrong. We didn't see how completely standards-based reform would turn into a basic-skills testing frenzy or the negative impact that it would have on educational quality. (Finn & Ravitch, 2007, p. 6)

7. NCLB depends on schools alone to eliminate the achievement gap. NCLB testing begins in third grade. This is the biggie. This ignores the child's prenatal care, first 5 or 6 years of life, and first 2 years of schooling. As we shall see in the chapter on learning, all of these years have an enormous impact on stimulating or stifling a child's potential. As noted above, a diverse coalition of educators has banded together to insist that any federal program address other factors, such as health and social well-being, that affect a child's ability and willingness to learn what the school tries to teach (www. boldapproach.org).

As "7+," we might note that the law presents a false dichotomy not recognized by any psychologist, cognitive scientist, or educator: you're either proficient or you're left behind. If the passing score on a test is 80, is a child who scores 79 left behind? The question answers itself.

A summary of the sanctions contained in NCLB: First year a school fails to make AYP, it is put on a list of "needs improvement" schools. Second year, it must offer students the option to go to a "successful" school. This sanction has backfired. It is supposed to help the neediest students in a "failing" school. A number of superintendents have told me it is the brightest kids who leave, and this was formally reported in 2007 in Broward County, Florida:

> The students with the lowest reading and math scores are getting left behind because the law gives students of underperforming schools the choice of going elsewhere, the Broward School District reported Monday. The brain drain has occurred at about 60 schools, where many of the brightest students have transferred out, taking with them federal money used to educate poor students. (Johnson, 2007)

Third year, it must provide free tutoring or other "supplemental services" to students. A boon for for-profit education firms. This sequencing makes no sense. Why let the students change schools after 2 years, but provide them with extra help in year 3? In the original draft bill, after 3 years in a failing school, the students were to be offered vouchers to attend private schools. It is a political expedient. Senator Edward Kennedy and other Democrats blocked the voucher proposals, and the supplemental services provision was a compromise. Fourth year, corrective action, which means the district takes more control of decision making and management. Fifth year, the school must undergo "restructuring" which could mean letting teachers go, letting principals go, reorganizing the school, or bringing in a private management firm.

So far, according to Robert Tomsho of *The Wall Street Journal,* those schools in restructuring aren't doing much of anything, nor are they exiting this category of failed schools (Tomsho, 2008). Tomsho reports that the GAO finds 40% of the 1,300 schools in restructuring aren't doing anything and another 40% have checked the "other" option, a convenient loophole (Tomsho, 2008).

A wonderful summary of the toxic outcomes of NCLB and high-stakes testing in general can be found in *When Childhood Collides with NCLB,* by Susan Ohanian (2008). Ohanian uses one column of each page to write an epic, free-verse poem about the disaster of NCLB. She uses the other column for quotes. Some quotes from the likes of the Business Roundtable and Achieve, Inc., support NCLB and testing, some repudiate it. In the end, though, her book makes NCLB look stupid and dangerous, which it is.

"This should change your life," says teacher/author James Herndon about reading (1971, p. 155). Read Ohanian's book. It might not change your life because you are already reading *this* book, which makes similar arguments in a less artful fashion. Give Ohanian's book to someone who needs it, like any NCLB supporter.

Neal McCluskey, a policy analyst at the libertarian think tank, Cato Institute, wrote,

> Republicans passed the No Child Left Behind Act, the most intrusive federal education law in American history. Five years later, with NCLB up for reauthorization, they can't jump ship fast enough....In the end neither Republicans nor Democrats should fight for NCLB. It hasn't helped either party, and it has hurt children all over the country. (2007)

Public school advocate Jamie Vollmer had a more succinct take: No Child Left Behind is "taking us straight to hell" (in Martin, J., 2007).

Perhaps the saddest commentary came from Congressman George Miller (D-CA), one of the Democrats who made the law possible. Watching Miller fight for NCLB was like watching someone bail with a pail to keep the Titanic afloat. Finally, he gave up:

> We didn't get it all right when we enacted the law. Throughout our schools and communities, the American people have a very strong sense that the No Child Left Behind Act is not fair. That it is not flexible. And that is not funded....I can tell you that there are no votes in the U. S. House of Representatives for continuing the No Child Left Behind Act without making serious changes to it...I have always said that I am proud to be one of the original coauthors of the No Child Left Behind Act. But what I really want is to be the proud coauthor of a law that works. (Miller, G., 2007)

Miller apparently didn't realize the damning implications of his last sentence.

Some of us argued from the beginning that NCLB was a plan to destroy American public education and privatize it. At the beginning, even as Bush moved to privatize everything else, we critics of NCLB were pooh-poohed. "How do you explain the backing of liberals such as Ted Kennedy and George Miller?" people asked whenever I made this case. My answer was always twofold: first, their staffs had failed them terribly. When I expressed my analysis to Alice Cain on Miller's staff, all she said was, "I certainly hope not."

Second, I thought President Bush had duped Senator Kennedy. In addition, Senator Kennedy knew he didn't have the votes to stop the bill—the most he could do was kill the voucher provisions and replace them with supplemental services. The bill called for much more money than Bush ever put up, and Kennedy began criticizing the law on that ground almost immediately after it passed, not realizing, apparently, that no amount of money could make the law work.

The kind of teaching and assessment system we have now resem bles Herndon's description of "the old German notion of apprenticeship; this year you get a nail; next year you get a hammer; the next you get to hit the nail with the hammer. I know that is crazy and the kids know it is crazy and the Germans know it is crazy, but we also know that is how things are, even if we don't know how they got that way or who decided it" (Herndon, 1971, p. 70). It doesn't have to be "that way" and we can decide to do it differently. I presented Chris Gallagher's general model of "engagement" on page 71. Consider Gallagher's model applied specifically to assessment:

Figure 4.2. Gallagher's Model Applied to Assessment	
Accountability	**Engagement**
Threat	Opportunity
Top-down	Bottom-up or inside-out
Policy tool	Instructional tool
High stakes	High impact
Standardized tests	Teacher-designed assessments
Assessment *of* learning	Assessment *for* learning
Assessment-driven instruction	Instruction-driven assessment
Event-based	Ongoing-embedded
Students subjected	Students involved

As noted earlier, most assessments do not assess learning, but instead achievement, which is confounded with family and community variables. Growth models attempt to assess actual learning, but fall short because they don't account for the large amount of time a student is out of school, both during the school year and over the summer. A recent study did try to measure what the researchers called *impact:* measuring the rate of learning when the students are in school vs. when they are not (Downey et al., 2008). The three approaches—achievement, learning, and impact—give different outcomes. Some schools with low achievement look better when evaluated on learning. Some schools look different when evaluated on impact than they do on either achievement or learning. They might be high- or low-impact schools (in the latter case, meaning a lot of loss when students are out of school). It is too early in the development of this procedure to determine if it can be applied to individual schools, but the distinction—achievement vs. learning vs. impact—is an important one.

PART II

This book is, by intent, a relatively small book even though its topics could easily give rise to a tome. Its purpose is not to lay out a plan, but to stimulate thought and discussion and, then, perhaps, action. Dewey felt that planning could never be more than tentative and short term because you could never really know how a person's experience with something might affect ensuing needs and experiences.

This section of the book presents some old research, as in the Eight-Year Study, and some contemporary work, as in the discussion of biogenetic research. The idea is not to present these efforts as *models* but to present them as exciting notions that would lift people off their fannies and stop them talking about the stupefying ideas that dominate education "discourse" today—national standards, high school exit exams, algebra for all, competition in the global economy, and getting kids ready for jobs. It hopes to make a national motto from the pre-Gerstner slogan of IBM, which the post-Gerstner IBM has apparently readopted: THINK.

In this section you will find:

- Using the reaction to *A Nation at Risk*, chapter 5 debunks the myth that America is trailing behind the world in science, mathematics, and engineering.

- Chapter 6 outlines the "10 Golden Rules for Competitiveness" developed by the Institute for Management Development followed by discussion of the World Economic Forum's "12 Pillars of Competitiveness" and where the U.S. ranks on each pillar.

- Centered on recent biogenetic research resolving the debate of nature vs. nurture, chapter 7 provides a discussion of the role of poverty and its extensive influence on student achievement. Nobel Laureate economist James Heckman outlines 15 issues of how poverty impacts children and youth; they are summarized in this chapter.

- Chapter 8 provides a brief discussion of recent research on insight and of Howard Gardner's exposition of multiple intelligences. It goes on to discuss how the Key School in Indianapolis, Indiana, utilized Gardner's work as its foundation.

- In John Goodlad's 1979 book *What Schools Are For*, he presents 12 "Goals for Schooling in the United States." Chapter 9 contains these 12 goals along with commentary on how these goals, penned in 1979, apply to education today.

- Chapter 10 offers highlights from an often misrepresented study, the Eight-Year Study. The lessons learned from this study remain relevant for education today, and are great discussion starters for how we can move past the criticism of America's schools.

- The final chapter presents three essays from the September 2008 issue of *Phi Delta Kappan*. Richard Gibboney, Nel Noddings, and Deborah Meir present their ideas for how schools should support democracy and how democracy should support schools.

Chapter 5:
Science, Engineering, and Economic Competitiveness

"Our students' performance today is the best indicator of our competitiveness tomorrow" (National Governors Association, 2006). So said Raymond Scheppach, executive director of the National Governors Association at a December, 2006, convening of a group to bemoan the most recent PISA results and, of course, to accept them uncritically. Our current economic crisis looks to be more a failure of business schools to moderate their students' greed, to endow them with appropriate ethics, and to teach an appropriate appreciation of risk vs. return than of the secondary schools to impart math and science. However, the quote above reveals the principal rationale for schooling these days: economic competitiveness.

As noted earlier, during the cold war, CIA chief Allen Dulles claimed that the Russians were producing more than twice as many mathematicians, scientists, and engineers as the U. S. When *Sputnik* went up, followed by other Sputniks and American satellites, one good thing happened—science became sexy. Before, the most common free association to "scientists" was "odd." I imagine the word "mad" was on a lot of lips as well. Scientists worked in isolation, often to no good end. Unfortunatley, the atomic bombing of Hiroshima and Nagasaki killed a lot of people's faith in the ability of science to lead the planet to the good life.

Sputnik said to many Americans that we had frittered away our science advantage with our materialistic way of life and we had to return to the scientific fold. A banker said, "If *Sputnik* can't make us realize how unimportant are our desires for color television, can it make us realize the possibility of the loss of all television, except perhaps the few programs monitored and fed to us by Communist zealots?" (Dickson, 2001, p. 139). William Manchester concluded, "*Sputnik 1* dealt the *coup de grace* to Ford's fading Edsel, which had been introduced the month before, and which was now widely regarded as a discredited symbol of the tinny baubles America must thrust aside" (Dickson, 2001, p. 140).

Sputnik led to some other important things too—the Interstate Highway System and ARPANET, the prototype for the Internet. But its impact on math, science, and engineering was almost immediate, especially through the National Defense Education Act. Its impact on K-12 was less successful, leading to the development of New Math and some other "new"s that were soon abandoned.

A Nation at Risk focused on high school and did not address the issue of scientists and engineers directly, but its examples of "The Risk" all had to do with engineered products.

> The risk is not only that the Japanese make automobiles more efficiently than Americans...It is not just that the South Koreans recently built the world's most efficient steel mill, or that American machine tools, once the pride of the world are being displaced by German products. (National Commission on Excellence in Education, 1983, pp. 6-7)

The Commission then went on to describe another phenomenon that today is encapsulated in a single word: globalization.

I was a high school senior when *Sputnik* entered orbit. I cannot remember a time since when anyone has said "we have enough scientists and engineers." Even during the "*Sputnik* Spike"—when masses of engineers were churned out by universities—discussion was in terms of playing catch-up to the Russians.

Fear as the Driving Force Behind "Reform"

Since *Sputnik*, the driving force of this country, especially in education, has been fear. From "the Russians are coming" through the *inevitable* economic dominance of Japan, through 9/11 and now the dreadnoughts of China and India, Americans have been told to be afraid, be very afraid. Instill enough fear in people and you can control people, to get them to act in something other than their best interests, to make them accept policies and actions that they might otherwise resist such as the Vietnam and Iraq wars (recall that in George Orwell's *1984*, Big Brother controlled potential rebels by confronting them with what they feared most).

In fact, the impending shortage of scientists and engineers is one of the longest running hoaxes in the country. It has been given credibility by the prestige of the National Science Foundation (NSF) in the 1980s and sustained today by many conservative individuals and groups, including the National Association of Manufacturers. These worthies are supposed to be free market advocates, but when they ask Congress to increase the number of H1B visas for high-skill foreigners, they are essentially saying that they don't want to compete in a free market, they want Uncle Sam to subsidize them: the foreigners will work for less than American-bred engineers.

The logic of the unpublished study (predicting a horrific shortage of engineers) by NSF policy analysist Peter House went like this:

- The participation of 22-year-olds in doctoral programs in science and engineering will remain stable.

- There will be a decline in the number of 22-year-olds after 1986.

- Given a stable participation rate, and a declining population of 22-year-olds, there will be a shortage of Ph.Ds.

It's not clear where House got his total number, but it came out that by 2006, it would amount to 675,000 people. Amazingly, this number stuck and was repeated by well-known people including Richard Atkinson, then president of the American Association for the Advancement of Science, and Robert Rosensweig, president of the American Association of Universities (Weinstein, n.d.).

To be sure, some people saw the flaw in this argument: it examines only the supply of scientists and engineers, and does not mention the demand for their services. Michigan Congressman Howard Wolpe had this to say:

The NSF study projected a shortfall of scientists and engineers without considering the future demand for such individuals in the marketplace. It simply observed a decline in the number of 22-year-olds and projected that this demographic trend would result in a huge shortfall. This could be termed the supply-side theory of labor market analysis. But making labor market projections without considering the demand side of the equation *doesn't pass the laugh test with experts in the field*. (Weinstein, n.d., emphasis added)

David Berliner and Bruce Biddle debunked the study in *The Manufactured Crisis* (Berliner & Biddle, 1995). George Will also saw the fallacious reasoning.

There is a crisis of overproduction of Ph.Ds and underconsumption of scholarship. To save money, schools rely increasingly on "gypsy scholars" drawn from the reserve army of unemployed Ph.Ds. They are hired on short-term contracts to teach but are not on the tenure track and are denied healthcare and other benefits.

Twenty years ago, 25% of all faculty members were part time. Today 42% are. For example, the *Chronicle of Higher Education* reports that in 1992 the California State University at Hayward had 407 tenured or tenure-track professors and 142 other lecturers, and by 1995, the numbers were 373 and 330 respectively (Will in Weinstein, n.d.).

Like many other things that ain't so (like, for instance, test scores are falling), the myth of the shortage lingers on. In 1991, Sloan Foundation demographer Michael Teitelbaum testified before Congress that no shortage existed. In 1996, he debunked the myth in *The New York Times* (Teitelbaum, 1996). And in 2007, there he was again testifying to Congress that study after study found no shortage:

> Unemployment among scientists and engineers remains much lower than for low-skilled workers, as it does for all highly educated workers. Nonetheless, tens of thousands of highly skilled professionals (scientists, engineers, computer experts) have been laid off by such companies as IBM, AT&T, Lockheed, and Grumman, and job prospects for recently minted scientists and engineers have plummeted.
>
> It is an employers' market. In much of the United States, stagnant or declining salaries have been the trend. For instance, from 1968 to 1994, the salary for an engineer with 10 years of experience declined 13% as measured in constant dollars. (Teitelbaum, 1996)

Not only have wages fallen, which they wouldn't if demand were higher than supply, universities have found themselves afflicted by a new disease: adjunctivitis. Adjunct professors, I can tell you from experience, make peanuts compared to those with regular positions. In addition, people with doctorates often stay on at universities as low-paid research assistants, leading long-time science writer, Dan Greenberg, to invent a new university position: post-doc emeritus.

In *The Chronicle of Higher Education,* Richard Monastersky observed that it takes a half-year longer now to get a doctorate than in 1987 and that nearly 70% of new physics grads take temporary positions, compared to 43% in 2000. Students see their professors spending more time writing grants (and being turned down), see post-doctorates who can't get a tenure-track position, and head elsewhere (Monastersky, 2007).

Greenberg, who has a savage wit, asks this rhetorical question:

> Why are so many science jobs and student slots in the U.S. filled
> by foreigners? For the same reason jobs in lettuce fields and
> apple orchards are filled by foreigners. Many qualified Ameri-
> cans shun science because, far more than the drum beaters
> for research let on, science can be a risky, unrewarding career
> choice…No amount of improved high school science is going
> to fix this problem, which is essentially economic. A doubling
> of salaries and improved conditions for getting ahead in a scien-
> tific career would bring in many more American recruits. But
> that's not going to happen. Despite the glorification of science,
> the marketplace sets the value and the price. Which is why
> foreigners flock to our schools and labs while Americans seek
> their fortunes in other fields. (2007)

Even so, America churns out about three scientists and engineers
(S&E) for every one new position in those fields (not counting
openings due to retirements). That's the finding of Lindsey Lowell of Georgetown University and Harold Salzman of the Urban
Institute. These researchers found some even more disturbing statistics: within 2 years, 20% of the graduates were in school, but not
in S&E programs. Forty-five percent were in the workforce, but
not in S&E positions. That's a combined 65% attrition rate in less
than 24 months—in 2 years (Lowell & Salzman, 2007). And people worry about the attrition of teachers—about 50% in 5 years.

Lowell and Salzman confirm Greenberg's contentions about
working conditions, and Monastersky's observation that the prestigious journal, *Nature,* called the condition of newly graduated
scientists, "indentured labour" (*Nature,* 2007). However, not only
is there not a decline, the number of citizens or permanent resi-
dents getting S&E degrees grew by a third, from 300,000 in 1972

to 400,000 in 2002. They found that between 1982 and 1998 the number of science and mathematics credits obtained by high school graduates had grown. And when they interviewed students who had abandoned S&E college programs, it was not because the kids couldn't cut it, but because they didn't like the quality of instruction.

Lowell and Salzman observe that discussion of who is number one among countries typically takes place in terms of average scores. But, as discussed on page 61, there is great variability around the mean, and given the demand-side weakness, there are plenty of able people to fill jobs. And, they note, policy discussions are always in terms of math and science, but "there is no substantial evidence to support the assertion that a nation's average levels of math and science mastery lead to a disproportionate share of innovation or economic growth" (Lowell & Salzman, 2007).

Salzman also testified recently before Congress and reported some results from interviews with employers:

> The skills science, technology, engineering and math job applicants and workers lack are communication skills that enable employees to work across boundaries, coordinate and integrate technical activities, navigate the multidisciplinary nature of today's work...A broad education that incorporates a range of technical and social science and humanities knowledge is important for developing a globally competitive workforce. In this, the United States currently has an advantage over the emerging economies. (Salzman, 2007)

Yet the charade continues. Lowell and Salzman's article is called "Into the Eye of the Storm." No doubt the title is a slam directed against a recent report from the National Academies that perpetuates the myth of the shortage, *Rising Above the Gathering Storm* (National Academics, 2007). It is pretentious[12] and dishonest and a barely disguised attempt to grab money. It worked. In late 2007, Congress passed the "America Competes" bill, designed, in part, to produce more mathematicians, engineers, and scientists. It has never been funded although the U.S. Department of Education says that states should use their funds from the American Recovery and Reinvestment Act of 2009 to further its goals (U.S. Department of Education, 2009).

Here's a slightly different take on any problem we might have competing: "The real trouble with this country is that we can't compete because by and large we have terrible boards of directors. I know because I'm on seven of them. They are dysfunctional for the most part. They should have accountability" (Nocera, 2007). That was Carl Icahn talking to *New York Times* business writer, Joe Nocera. But until now, accountability was for the public sector, especially public schools; the private sector was busy taking care of us by building Bush's "ownership society." If I were Black or Hispanic, I'd probably see the current foreclosure and bailout mess as a deliberate plan to redistribute wealth back to White people.

---

12   The title alludes to Winston Churchill's *The Gathering Storm*, his chronicle of events leading up to World War II.

Chapter 6:
The Real Meaning of Competition

So what is the point of having all these mathematicians, engineers, and scientists? The post-*Sputnik* panic was a reaction to a genuine threat that could have obliterated the globe. Now, the threat is the rise of China and India, economically, and a concern over our ability to compete in that omnipresent ogre, the global economy.

What exactly does that mean, "compete in the global economy?" The process is seldom defined, but it is typically presented as a zero-sum game. If China and India win, we lose. Actually, if China and India win, we win, too. It makes no sense to hope that the two largest nations in the world remain largely in the doldrums of poverty. New York City Mayor Michael Bloomberg got it right when he said:

> While we should recognize that China and the United States are competitors, we should also understand that geopolitics and global economics are not zero-sum games. Just as a growing American economy is good for China, a growing Chinese economy is good for America. That means we have a stake in working together to solve common problems, rather than trying to browbeat or intimidate the other into action. (2007)

Right. The United States invented the microchip. The whole world has benefited. Who cares if an AIDS vaccine is invented in Nigeria or Nebraska? No one should. Bloomberg's statement is true but it doesn't get us to the nub of competitiveness.

Moreover, Sam Walton is at least as much responsible as scientists and engineers for American competitiveness, according to Amar Bhidé of the Columbia Business School:

> America's competitive advantage resides mainly in its creative use of information technology, especially in the large and growing services sector, led by companies like Walmart. Walmart and its followers are as much a part of the technological success of America as Silicon Valley...And our supply of high-level science and ideas in most fields far exceeds our capacity to use it. (in Lohr, 2008)

So what is "competitiveness?" As I said, few talk about it. Wikipedia defines it and immediately repudiates the definition: "Competitiveness is a comparative concept of the ability of a firm, subsector or country to sell and supply goods and/or services in a given market. Although widely used in economics and business management, the usefulness of the concept, particularly in the context of national competitiveness, is vigorously disputed by economists such as Paul Krugman" (Wikipedia, n.d.). Well, Krugman is hardly alone.

The Lausanne, Switzerland-based Institute for Management Development (IMD) ranks 55 nations on their competitiveness each year (IMD, 2008a). The United States has been number one since 1994, when it displaced Japan.

IMD uses over 300 criteria to establish its rankings—which should give you some idea of how complex the concept is. IMD collapses these criteria into four factors: economic performance, government efficiency, business efficiency, and infrastructure. Each of these criteria contains five subfactors (see Figure 6.1).

Figure 6.1. IMD's Criteria for Competitiveness			
Economic Performance	Government Efficiency	Business Efficiency	Infrastructure
Domestic Economy	Public Finance	Productivity	Basic Infrastructure
International Trade	Fiscal Policy	Labor Market	Technological Infrastructure
International Business	Institutional Framework	Finance	Scientific Infrastructure
Employment	Business Legislation	Management Practices	Health and Environment
Prices	Societal Framework	Attitudes and Values	Education

Note that education is only 1 of 20 subfactors. Of course, the subfactors are not independent. Education bears on scientific and technological infrastructure, for instance, as well as productivity and attitudes and values (IMD, 2008b).

IMD also has developed 10 "Golden Rules of Competitiveness":

1. Create a stable and predictable legislative environment.
2. Work on a flexible and resilient economic structure.
3. Invest in traditional and technological infrastructure.
4. Promote savings and domestic investment.

5. Develop aggressiveness on the international markets as well as attractiveness for direct foreign investment.

6. Focus on quality, speed, and transparency in government and administration.

7. Maintain a relationship between wage levels, productivity, and taxation.

8. Preserve the social fabric by reducing wage disparity and strengthening the middle class.

9. Invest heavily in education, especially at the secondary level, and in the life-long training of the labor force.

10. Balance the economies of proximity and globality to ensure substantial wealth creation, while preserving value systems that citizens share. (IMD, 2008b)

The Research and Knowledge page of IMD's Web site wonders how long the U.S. can be number one (IMD, 2008b). It draws attention to the fact that Singapore has been rising fast and is second (even if it overtakes the U.S., its size, about the same population as the Baltimore-Washington Metro area, must be taken into account). Perhaps more important, Japan was number one in 1989 when IMD began its rankings. Japan's decline

> followed a period of economic boom, real estate price follies, and exuberant assets expansion. In addition, the liberalization of financial instruments took place without the appropriate regulatory environment; corporate governance was inadequate with little accountability and transparency; and the government was quickly overwhelmed by the magnitude of the crisis. (IMD, 2008c)

Sound familiar? It should. About the only difference is that our government was not overwhelmed. It came closer to being paralyzed. It was perversely slow to figure out what was going on and in the spring of 2009, it still apears to be improvising. The article notes that the U.S. economy is unusually open and resilient while Japan's traditions made it difficult to change *anything* (I also recall an NPR segment in the late 1980s saying that Japan's banks had such obsolescent technology they could not possibly *know* how big their debts were). But the article contends that "A recession in the U.S. is a strong possibility. Will it last and will it spread? In both cases, the answer is probably yes" (IMD, 2008c). The answers are now known: yes to both.

The better known World Economic Forum (WEF) also annually ranks nations in its *Global Competitiveness Report.* Again, the U.S. was number one among the 131 nations ranked in the 2007-2008 report (WEF, 2007); it's number one among 134 nations in the 2008-2009 report (WEF, 2008). Hundreds of variables go into the WEF's rankings, too. It then condenses them to the "Twelve Pillars of Competitiveness" (see Figure 6.2).

Figure 6.2. Twelve Pillars of Competitiveness	
1. Infrastructure	7. Labor Market Efficiency
2. Institutions	8. Financial Market
3. Macroeconomy	Sophistication
4. Health and Primary	9. Technological Readiness
Education	10. Market Size
5. Higher Education	11. Business Sophistication
and Training	12. Innovation
6. Goods Market Efficiency	

The WEF's approach is unabashedly materialist, capitalist, and worshipful towards business, but it defines competitiveness by what countries do for their citizens in terms of improving standards of living and productivity. We can see this definition operating in the high rankings awarded to Denmark (3rd), Sweden (4th), Finland (6th), and Norway (16th) (tell me again about how socialism is dead). These countries carry tax burdens that American conservatives are always yammering about, accusing them of being Nanny-states. And, indeed, the 2007-2008 WEF ranks these nations 110th, 126th, 115th, and 64th, respectively, in terms of "extent and effect of taxation." In the eyes of the WEF, the social programs, the social safety net provided by these countries overcomes their high tax rates.

A detailed discussion of the twelve pillars of competitiveness and America's rank on each follows.

1. INFRASTRUCTURE (6th).Until recently, Americans probably didn't think of infrastructure as relating to competitiveness because they take it so much for granted. Or did. Then Hurricane Katrina destroyed the Gulf Coast, and a bridge between Minneapolis and St. Paul, Minnesota, fell into the Mississippi. Then, the rivers of Iowa breeched their levees. Now we know different. To move goods and services effectively you need a good system of ports, airports, highways, and rail lines. You also need a reliable supply of electricity (ask any Iraqi) and a solid, extensive, and rapid telecommunications network. The Chinese response to the earthquake in Szechuan in 2008 makes our response to Hurricane Katrina

look like the effort of a fourth-world nation (except, of course, in the reaction to all those schools that fell down when other buildings didn't—China quickly clamped censorship on reporting about that).

Beyond that, there is what journalist Rick Perlstein calls "e. coli conservatism." It is deadly because e. coli conservatives won't spend the money to take care of the infrastructure. The Minnesota legislature passed legislation for more money for roads and bridges. Governor Pawlenty vetoed it. Then the bridge fell down, the legislature passed a new $6.6 billion transportation bill, and Pawlenty vetoed it, calling the plan "ridiculous." The legislature overrode the veto (Kaszuba & Brunswick, 2008). The legislature also approved a $39 million compensation package, that Pawlenty signed, for victims of the collapse.

This is e. coli conservatism. If you don't maintain proper oversight of the infrastructure and spend enough money to keep it in good repair, you get sick or die from e. coli in your spinach and beef, and salmonella in your poultry, eggs, jalapeños, and peanut products—and your bridges fall down.

2. INSTITUTIONS (33rd). In some countries you can't avail yourself of the amenities of life without a kickback or bribe. The WEF is clear: "Excessive bureaucracy and red tape, overregulation, corruption, dishonesty in dealing with public contracts or the political independence of the judiciary system pose significant economic costs and slow down the process of economic development" (2008, p. 4).

The corporate scandals of the last few years have signaled how important accounting and reporting standards are in the private sector. If private institutions lack honesty and ethical behavior, consumers and investors alike lose confidence. Nothing illustrates this better than the subprime mortgage scandal wherein assessors approved ludicrously high values of homes, if they assessed them at all, and loan agencies made loans to people they *knew* couldn't repay them. Or in some cases they didn't know because they didn't bother to run a credit check. Then the banks bundled the mortgages—securitized them—and sold them like stocks and tried to keep themselves safe by buying "insurance" in the form of credit default swaps.

3. MACROECONOMIC STABILITY (75th). We look awful on this pillar. The only saving graces have been low loan rates and the falling dollar. The WEF hates budget and trade deficits. Money paid as interest on debt is not available to improve productivity or citizens' lives. Ironically, despite the falling dollar and despite sending more goods as exports than we bought as imports, the trade deficit in June 2008, hit an all-time high. The culprit at the time: Oil prices. The price of oil more than offset our record exports. Currently, oil is down and the dollar has partially recovered, but President Obama's recovery initiatives will, at least in the short term, enlarge the deficit.

4. HEALTH AND PRIMARY EDUCATION (34th). W. Norton Grubb of the University of California examined the nature of inequality (and lack of it) in Finland (Grubb, 2007). He and his team canvassed the country. They did not find one instance of children not being able to attend school because

of chronic health problems. In some urban slum areas of the U.S., asthma is epidemic, as is lead poisoning. A UNICEF study ranked the U.S. 20th of 21 wealthy nations in taking care of its children. It's mostly poor children, of course, who get little attention until there's a scandal. I doubt any state or federal legislator paid much attention to this issue until a 12-year-old boy died because his mother couldn't find someone who would extract his infected tooth (Otto, 2007). The U.S. is 32nd in infant mortality and 84th in the incidence of AIDS, two of the subfactors of health and primary education. Primary education is itself ranked 28th.

5. HIGHER EDUCATION AND TRAINING (5th). Part of this high ranking no doubt stems from the high esteem in which the world holds American institutions of higher education. But this high ranking also would seem to reflect a change in attitudes towards training by business and industry. Both the Secretary's Commission on Achieving Necessary Skills (U.S. Department of Labor, 1992) and the Sandia Report (Carson et al., 1993) took business and industry to task for how little money American business spent on training compared to expenditures in other countries. Both also noted that training money was overwhelmingly spent on already-skilled workers, compared to more egalitarian distributions in other nations. The U.S. ranks 11th on the subpillar "extent of staff training."

6. GOODS MARKET EFFICIENCY (12th). The WEF says, "Countries with efficient goods markets are positioned to produce the right mix of goods and services given supply-and-

demand market conditions, and such markets also ensure that these goods can be most effectively traded in the economy" (2008, p. 5). This means that healthy domestic and international competition are needed to make sure that companies stay lean and mean—efficient. The customer has a role to play here—people who accept shoddy goods and services don't push companies to be honest and efficient. If we're ranked 12th, though, is there a need for Angie's list or publications like *Pocketbook*, both of which seem to be doing quite well?

7.   LABOR MARKET EFFICIENCY (1st). In addition to the right goods, you need to make sure you have the right people in the right jobs and that they have incentives to put forth their best effort. To me, more than any other pillar, this one treats workers as cogs in the business machine. It also lets CEOs off the hook. It says nothing about how CEOs have exploited the compensation process and were paid huge sums even when the company is not profitable and the stock price declines. See Bebchuk and Fried's *Pay Without Performance: The Unfilled Promise of Executive Compensation* (Bebchuck & Fried, 2004).

8.   FINANCIAL MARKET SOPHISTICATION (11th). So-phisticated financial markets make capital available for investments through a sound banking system, well-regulated securities exchanges, and venture capital. Remember, a rank is not a score. For health and primary education, the U.S. received a rank of 34th with a score of 6.0 (out of 7). For Market Sophistication, the U.S. ranks 11th, but with a score of only 5.7. This means a lot of countries are in a sorry state on this pillar.

9. TECHNOLOGICAL READINESS (9th). The WEF contends that:

> Whether the technology used has or has not been invented within its borders is immaterial for our purposes in analyzing competitiveness....It does not matter whether a country has invented electricity, the Internet, or the airplane. What is important is that these inventions are available to the business community. (WEF, 2008, p. 5)

I have heard tales from friends traveling abroad that our use of broadband here is pathetic compared to parts of Europe. The top five countries are, in order, Sweden, Iceland, Switzerland, Netherlands, and Denmark, followed by Hong Kong, Korea, and Norway (pp. 18-19).

10. MARKET SIZE: I have omitted this pillar. The WEF itself admits that some contradictory data weaken the claim that this is a pillar on par with the other 11.

11. BUSINESS SOPHISTICATION (7th). "Business sophistication is conducive to higher efficiency in the production of goods and services. This leads, in turn, to increased productivity, thus enhancing a nation's competitiveness" (WEF, 2008, p. 6). Businesses have to be ready to adopt new inventions, to be of high quality themselves and to have high-quality networks among them.

12. INNOVATION (1st—But not much longer if NCLB hangs around). This, in WEF's view, is the most critical pillar of all because it is the only one that doesn't eventually lead to

diminishing returns. Building bigger or faster airplanes can only improve developed countries' productivity so much. Improving existing technologies and goods and markets is very important to less-developed nations, but for highly developed nations, innovation is crucial.

> Firms in these [innovative] countries must design and develop cutting-edge products and processes to maintain a competitive edge. This requires an environment that is conducive to innovative activities supported by both public and private sectors.In particular this means sufficient investment in research and development especially by private, high-quality research universities, collaboration in research between universities and industry, and the protection of intellectual property. (WEF, 2008, p. 6)

Of course, the collaboration efforts carry some risk, especially in an area like drug research where studies financed by pharmaceutical companies are much more likely to find results favorable to a company's products than are studies that are financed through some independent agency.

I will point out here, and discuss later, that Robert Sternberg, Dean of Arts and Sciences at Tufts University, has written that, in our obsession with testing, we have produced one of the best instruments in the nation's history for stifling creativity (Sternberg, 2006).

As with the IMD factors, these pillars are interrelated. Market and labor efficiencies cannot be developed in countries that have poorly developed infrastructure or where social connections play a bigger role than merit and skill.

Still we can see, given the complexity of competitiveness as conceptualized by either the IMD or WEF and visible to all in the ruins of the global economy, those who would lay the burden of competitiveness on the schools are fools and liars. This is a good time to recall the words of the education historian, Lawrence Cremin, written when we were in thrall to Japan and just before Japan's bubble burst:

> American economic competitiveness with Japan and other nations is to a considerable degree a function of monetary, trade and industrial policy, and of decisions made by the President and Congress, the Federal Reserve Board, and the Federal Departments of the Treasury, Commerce, and Labor. Therefore to conclude that problems of international competitiveness can be solved by educational reform, especially educational reform defined solely as school reform, is not merely utopian and millenialist, it is at best a foolish and at worst a crass effort to direct attention away from those truly responsible for doing something about competitiveness and to lay the burden instead on the schools. It is a device that has been used repeatedly in the history of American education. (1990, pp. 102-103)

Chapter 7:
"Poverty is Poison"[13]

Years ago I read an article about Duke Ellington in which he said he was loved so much as a baby, he was 2-years-old before his feet touched the ground. That might have been the source of his genius. The debate surrounding the nature-nurture controversy is over. Genes won. The environment won. Herrnstein and Murray were wrong. The outcome was a new view of nature and nurture captured in the phrase "gene expression."

Gene expression is something that has been known for a long time, but not used in education until recently, notably 2003. It's like an experiment many readers might have conducted in elementary school: sprout two genetically identical beans under different conditions and you get plants that are differentially healthy. Gene expression can be subtle and pervasive. I recall a story about some number of cloned cows—five I think—and the reporter noting that pigmentation can be affected by the location of the unborn calf in the womb—different places get different amount of nutrients that affect coloration.

When it came to research using twins and examining the sources of whatever it is that leads to high scores on IQ tests, the outcomes generally pointed to genes. Environment accounted for little variation. However, the typical method of study obscured

---

13　Borrowed from *New York Times* columnist Paul Krugman's column of the same title February 18, 2008.

environmental impacts. The studies were mostly correlational and childrens' IQs are correlated with their siblings' and parents' and tightly correlated with any identical twin.

But imagine this experiment: we find two parents with the same IQs and a newly arrived set of identical twins. The parents raise one twin and child development experts raise the other twin, providing every known kind of enrichment. At age 6, we have these IQ test results:

Parents IQ	Twin 1	Twin 2
100	100	130
101	101	131
102	102	132
103	103	133
104	104	134

It is pretty easy to see that the parents' IQ and those of Twin 1 are perfectly correlated. What about Twin 2? The parents and Twin 2 also have IQs that are perfectly correlated. Perfect correlation just means that as the scores on one variable change (parental IQ in this case), the scores on another variable change in a perfectly predictable way (childrens' IQs). That happens with both twins. The ringer, of course, is that the program of cognitive enrichment resulted in Twin 2 having an IQ that is two standard deviations above the parents'. Compared to the sample on which the test was normed, Twin 1's are around the 50th percentile, Twin 2's are around the 98th percentile. Correlational studies tend to favor genetic interpretations, while those that look at mean differences from different treatments show an environmental impact as well.

Eric Turkheimer of the University of Virginia was interested in the nature-nurture issue and noticed something about the actual twin studies: they included very few poor people (Richter, 2003; Turkheimer, Haley, D'Onofrio, Waldron, & Gottesman, 2004). Poor people don't volunteer for research studies.

To find a database with large numbers of poor people, Turkheimer and his colleagues accessed data from the National Perinatal Collaborative Project, a large epidemiological study from 1959 to 1974 involving 45,000 mothers and 55,000 children. The study included more poor families than occur in the population at large. The project administered a Wechsler IQ test to all children at age 7.

In Turkheimer's study, the relative influence of genes and environment differed dramatically according to the socioeconomic status of the parents. For affluent parents, it was mostly genes. For poor parents, environment accounted for 60% of the variance, a huge amount. This is an instance of gene expression—the resources of affluence allow a child to reach his or her full genetic potential in terms of IQ. The resource-poor environments of impoverished families squelch that potential.

Other research shows environmental influences as well. It's a long way from neurological research to the classroom, but the research does show that prolonged stress alters the architecture of the brain.

> Neural circuits for dealing with stress are particularly malleable (or 'plastic') during the fetal and early childhood periods. Early experiences shape how readily they are activated and how well they can be contained and turned off. Toxic stress during this

early period can affect developing brain circuits and hormonal systems in a way that leads to poorly controlled stress-response systems that will be overly-active and slow to shut down when faced with threats throughout the lifespan. (National Scientific Council on the Developing Child, 2006)

Although this publication, from the National Scientific Council on the Developing Child, doesn't make any link to classrooms, it doesn't seem much of a leap to associate prolonged early childhood stress to classroom behavior problems. The publication does link prolonged early childhood stress to depression, anxiety disorders, alcoholism, drug abuse, cardiovascular disease, diabetes, and stroke. Quite a lineup.

The good news is that interventions can help. Geneticists no longer speak of genes and environment in "either-or" terms. As the National Research Council reports, "Since parenting and other environmental influences can moderate the development of inherited tendencies in children, efforts to assist parents and other caregivers to sensitively read a child's behavioral tendencies and to create a supportive context for the child are worthwhile" (Shonkoff & Phillips, 2009, p. 43).

This perspective has generated a revolution in behavioral genetics. Sir Michael Rutter, professor of developmental psychopathology at the University of London, says, "I am skeptical that genetic work will ever provide an understanding of the basis of intelligence. It doesn't really matter whether the heritability of IQ is this particular figure or that one. Changing the environment can still make an enormous difference" (Kirp, 2007). (One must keep in mind that the "heritability" statistic applies only to the group on which it was calculated and only at that one point in time.)

As David Kirp puts it, "If heredity defines the limits of intelligence, the research shows, experience largely determines whether those limits will be reached. And if this is so, the prospects for remedying social inequalities may be better than we thought" (Kirp, 2007).

And, the further good news is that a good environment might perpetuate itself. When rat pups who had anxious mothers that were not providing proper care were given to mothers who did, the pups became less stressed. When these pups grew to have their own offspring, they were much more likely to provide proper care for their pups (Kirp, 2007).

The discussion is becoming more complicated. The November 11, 2008, science section of *The New York Times* asked "Are genes and DNA hopelessly outmoded concepts?" Carl Zimmer pointed out that scientists

> no longer conceive of a typical gene as a single protein. There are simply too many exceptions to the conventional rules for genes...the familiar double helix of DNA no longer has a monopoly on heredity. Other molecules clinging to DNA can produce striking differences between two organisms with the same genes. (2008, p. D1)

Natalie Angier took Zimmer's point farther and wrote that:

> DNA's chemical cousin, RNA [is] doing complicated things it wasn't supposed to do. Not long ago, RNA was seen as a bureaucrat, the middle molecule between a gene and a protein... Now we find cases of short clips of RNA acting like DNA, transmitting genetic secrets to the next generation directly, without bothering to ask permission. We find cases of RNA acting like a protein, catalyzing chemical reactions, pushing other molecules around or tearing them down. RNA is like the vice presidency: it's executive, it's legislative, it's furtive. (Angier, 2008, p. D2)

Stay tuned for more revolutions, but if I read these articles right, these new discoveries and those to come will take us farther and farther away from the determinism presumed in the old nature-nurture distinction.

Turkheimer is not sanguine that we will ever find a few key variables to ameliorate the impact of poverty. "It's the accumulation of many, many small things that together make poverty" (Martin, C. P., 2005). Head Start-like programs can help, but the biggest aid would be getting the kids out of poverty.

All of this is good news for advocates of preschool for low-income children. Nobel Laureate economist James J. Heckman provides a good summary of the issues—issues that go far beyond preschool. In their many papers, Heckman and his colleagues are prone to the old technique of "tell 'em what you're going tell 'em, tell 'em, tell 'em what you've told 'em." The following is his pre-paper summary of a recent paper, reprinted with permission (Heckman, 2008).

1. Many major economic and social problems such as crime, teenage pregnancy, dropping out of school, and adverse health conditions are linked to low levels of skill and ability in society.

2. In analyzing policies that foster skills and abilities, society should recognize the multiplicity of human abilities.

3. Currently public policy in the U.S. focuses on promoting and measuring cognitive ability through IQ and achievement tests. The accountability standards in the No Child Left Behind Act concentrate attention on achievement test scores and do not evaluate important noncognitive factors that promote success in school and life.

4. Cognitive abilities are important determinants of socioeconomic success.

5. So are socioemotional skills, physical and mental health, perseverance, attention, motivation, and self-confidence. They contribute to performance in society at large and even help determine scores on the very tests that are commonly used to measure cognitive achievement.

6. Ability gaps between advantaged and disadvantaged open up early in the lives of children.

7. Ability gaps of young children are major predictors of cognitive and socioemotional abilities, as well as a variety of other outcomes such as crime and health.

8. Family environments in the U.S. and many other countries in the world have deteriorated over the last 40 years.

9. Experimental evidence on the positive effects of early interventions on children in disadvantaged families is consistent with a large body of nonexperimental evidence showing that the absence of supporting family environments harms child outcomes.

10. If society intervenes early enough, it can improve cognitive and socioemotional abilities and the health of disadvantaged children.

11. Early interventions promote schooling, reduce crime, foster workforce productivity and reduce teenage pregnancy.

12. These interventions are estimated to have high benefit-cost ratios and rates of return.

13. As programs are currently configured, interventions early in the life cycle of disadvantaged children have much higher economic returns than later interventions such as reduced pupil-teacher ratios, public job training, convict rehabilitation programs, adult literacy programs, tuition subsidies, or expenditure on police.

14. Life cycle skill formation is dynamic in nature. Skill begets skill; motivation begets motivation. Motivation cross-fosters skill and skill cross-fosters motivation. If a child is not motivated to learn and engage early in life, the more likely it is

that when the child becomes an adult, it will fail in social and economic life. The longer society waits to intervene in the life cycle of a disadvantaged child, the more costly it is to remediate disadvantage.

15. A major refocus of policy is required to capitalize on knowledge about the life cycle of skill and health formation and the importance of the early years in creating equality in America, and in producing skills for the workforce.

Heckman's paper runs the gamut in scope from the neural to the societal. Its title, after all, is *Schools, Skills, and Synapses*.

Among exhibits in the paper is a photo of a cross section of two brains (done with imaging, not surgery). One brain shows normal development, the other shows the devastating impact on a child who was placed, as were many, in sensory-depriving Romanian state-operated orphanages. Heckman calls the conditions of these institutions "atrocious." In any case, the institutionalized child's brain is smaller than the normal brain (and, yes, size matters), its cortex shows atrophy, and its ventricles are enlarged.

Behavioral geneticists these days classify brain events as "experience expectant" and "experience dependent." Experience expectants are occurrences that a new brain expects, such as auditory stimulation and patterned light (Shonkoff & Phillips, 2000, p. 54). These orphans' brains were deprived of experiences their brains expected. They had degenerated and showed pathologies. The children later demonstrated cognitive problems, impairments in social behavior, and abnormal sensitivity to stress. The later they were adopted, the poorer their recovery from their deprivations.

We can note as an aside that the brain matures over a long period of time. Some cortical functions associated with reasoning do not mature until age 18 or 19. Could it be that most eighth-grade brains are not *ready* for algebra?

When I reflect on this research on brain maturation, I am always reminded of Thomas Jefferson writing.

> There is a certain period of life, say from eight to fifteen or sixteen years of age, when the mind, like the body, is not yet firm enough for laborious and close operations. If applied to such, it falls an early victim of premature exertion; exhibiting indeed at first, in these young and tender subjects, the flattering appearance of their being men while they are yet children, but ending in reducing them to be children when they should be men. (Jefferson, 1782 in Hammond et al., 2007)

Heckman contends that the proper measure of disadvantage is not necessarily family poverty or parental education. It is the quality of parenting. The National Research Council Institute of Medicine seems to agree:

> The inextricable transaction between biology and experience also contributes to a better understanding of developmental disorders and the effect of early intervention. Hereditary vulnerabilities establish probabilistic, not deterministic, developmental pathways that evolve in concert with the experiential stressors, or buffers, in the family, the neighborhood, and the school. That is why early experiences of abuse, neglect, poverty, and family violence are of such concern. They are likely to enlist the genetic vulnerabilities of some children into a downward spiral of progressive dysfunction. By contrast, when

children grow up in more supportive contexts, the hereditary vulnerabilities that some children experience may never be manifested in problematic behavior. Understanding the co-action of nature and nurture contributes to early prevention. (Shonkoff & Phillips, 2000)

So poverty is an "excuse" in that the environment of impoverished lives inhibits the full expression of a child's genetic potential, even altering the architecture of the brain.

The first person I ever heard say "poverty is not an excuse" was Lisa Graham Keegan, then state superintendent of Arizona public schools, at a large-scale assessment conference in Phoenix. Had I been in position, I would have lept onto the stage and said "I agree. Poverty is not an excuse. Poverty is a condition. It is like gravity, affecting everything you do on the planet." My way at the time, I guess, of calling it "an accumulation of small deprivations." The person I've most recently heard wave off the impact of poverty is District of Columbia Public Schools' Chancellor Michelle Rhee who, donning a scholarly mantle, called it "complete crap" (Fields, 2008).

For me, people who say poverty is not an excuse must then explain the extraordinary difference in test scores in this country between kids who attend low-poverty schools and kids who attend high-poverty schools. And they must also explain why countries that have large government programs to transfer wealth to the poor do not show as steep a socioeconomic test score gradient as the U. S. and some other countries.

That is, in all countries, test scores increase with increasing family socioeconomic status. But in places like Finland, as wealth increases, scores do not climb as steeply as in some other countries such as the U.S. Overall, the gradient in the U.S. is about average among the 30 countries that make up the OECD. The problem for the U.S. is that it has more poverty than any of the other OECD countries except Mexico. And that poverty shows up in test scores.

The U.S. Department of Education typically releases information on how schools with differing levels of poverty perform on international comparisons. We have to use a proxy variable for poverty, namely percentage eligibility for free and reduced price meals. It is a proxy that seems to work reasonably well in elementary and middle schools, but not high schools because high school students are loathe to admit they are poor.

Figure 7.1 depicts what one set of results looked like from PIRLS 2001 (NCES, 2003). The column to the far left is the percentage of students in the U.S. attending schools with the poverty level shown in the middle column (NCES, 2008b). The right-hand column shows the test scores of the students in the various categories.

The U.S. average of 542 soars well above the international average. Students in schools with the fewest students in poverty scored much higher than the highest nation, Sweden (Finland, a nation that typically scores high, did not participate in the study). So did students in 10-24.9% range of poverty, although not by

Figure 7.1. One Set of Results from PIRLS 2001		
% U.S. Students Attending	% Students in the School in Poverty*	Score
14.3	Less than 10	589
19.5	10-24.9	567
29.8	25-49.9	551
21.3	50-74.9	519
15.1	75 and more	485
U.S. Overall		542
Sweden (top among 35 nations)		561
International Average		500

*See note on Figure 7.2.

much. If the students in schools with 25-49.9% poverty constituted a nation, it would rank fourth among the 35 participating
nations.

I should point out that the students in the lowest-poverty schools
are not necessarily in wealthy schools, although no doubt some of
them are. All we know is that these schools have fewer than 10% of
the students in poverty. The other 90% could be blue collar, white
collar, affluent, or some combination thereof. We don't know.

Similar statistics exist for TIMSS, but not for PISA—PISA tests
15-year-olds and, as noted, high school students are reluctant to
admit to poverty. We *can* use another proxy variable—ethnicity.
Such a display shows once again, the large inequalities plaguing
schools and, thus, society (Baldi, Jin, Skemer, Green, & Hergett,
2007). See Figure 7.2.

Figure 7.2. PISA 2006 Results, Mathematics	
International Average*	500
Finland (#1)	548
U.S. Students	474
Whites	523
Blacks	409
Hispanics	439
Asians	499
American Indians/Alaska Natives	436
Native Hawaiian/Pacific Islander	483

*Note: The data for performance by poverty level and ethnicity come from chapters in both the 2003 and 2006 reports, "How Different Groups Perform." They were adapted by the author.

We see that kids who are not poor do well in international comparisons. White kids do well, often very well, even in mathematics which is invariably the U.S.'s worst subject. When the fearmongers unleash their propaganda machines, they invariably speak of an undifferentiated "American schools," but American schools are nothing if not differentiated by both ethnicity and wealth.

A new paper (Berliner, 2009) has emerged too recently to be integrated into the text of this chapter; however, the "out-of-school" factors that affect achievement in school merit mentioning here. Some of these factors have been covered in this book:

- Birth-weight and nongenetic prenatal influences
- Inferior medical care
- Food insecurity
- Pollutants

- Family relations and stress
- Neighborhood norms
- Poverty's effect on test scores
- Extended opportunities

Chapter 8:
A Few Words About Learning—Eureka!

W hen my elementary school teachers told us to "put on your thinking caps," they probably didn't realize that they were stunting our cognitive growth. Well, that's a little harsh. It would be more accurate to say that there should have been other times when they gave us really tough problems, either verbal or mathematical and said, "let your mind wander where it will for a while." Woolgathering leads to insights in a way that focused learning does not.

You want insights? If you've reached an impasse on a problem, sleep on it. Be sure, though, to set the alarm a few minutes ahead so you can lie there a little bit before the morning routine starts. Insight requires relaxation. Newton saw an apple fall (maybe). Archimedes took a bath. Friedrich Kekule had a daydream about a snake seizing its tail and emerged with the ring structure of benzene. Henri Poincaré invented the essence of nonEuclidean geometry while boarding a bus. I can't guarantee such important insights, but try it the next time you reach an impasse. Let go.

Don't seek insight by meditating, though, unless you're really, really good at it. Jonah Lehrer recounts the time a Zen meditator attempted a series of very hard test items known as Compound Remote Association Problems (CRAP). CRAP requires you to take three words, such as pine, crab, and sauce, and think of a word that can be combined with all three to form other words, in this case, apple (as the joke of the acronym became tired, the P of the tests was dropped) (Lehrer, 2008).

The Zen meditator couldn't get any of them, until, all of a sudden, he started getting them all in very quick order. Focusing your attention, as in meditation, decreases your chances for insight because insight requires relaxation. This particular meditator was good enough that he could focus on not being focused. How you relax is apparently idiosyncratic to at least some extent. Lehrer reports that Nobel laureate physicist, Richard Feynmann, preferred topless bars where he would sip 7UP® and, if an insight occurred, "scribble equations on cocktail napkins" (Lehrer, 2008, p. 44).

Not everyone believes that insight is a unique cognitive process. Some, usually referred to as business-as-usual theorists, think that the same processes are used for insight as for directed thought. Both the special process theorists and the business-as-usual theorists do agree that insight solutions differ from noninsight solutions in several ways:

> Problem solvers experience their solutions as sudden and obviously correct (the *Aha!*). However, problems solvers often reach an impasse before producing an insight solution and often cannot tell you how they reached their solution (Bowden, Jung-Beeman, Fleck, & Kounios, 2005). Subsequent EEG research has shown a burst of activity at the moment the *Aha!* arrives (the subject in the experiment pushes a button to tell the experimenters he's got it). This suggests that the *Aha!* is not an affective reaction to the solution that occurs later. (Kounios, Fleck, Green, Payne, Stevenson, Bowden, et.al., 2008)

It appears to arrive simultaneously with the solution.

People who prefer to solve problems by insight differ from those who prefer directed thinking: The resting brain-states of high insight people look different from those who do not approach problems insightfully, with the former showing more activity in the right hemisphere.

What does this mean for educators? Not much at the moment, and I offer this brief discussion only to indicate once again the impoverished view of the brain offered in most of today's schools.

The same may be said of other "brain-based education" schemes. *Phi Delta Kappan* ran a special section on brain-based education in February, 2008, and it illustrates two of the common problems with the field. First, Eric P. Jensen writes that "In a groundbreaking book, *Human Brain, Human Learning*, Leslie Hart argued, among other things, that cognitive processes were significantly impaired by classroom threat" (Jensen, 2008, p. 410). Yes, but we don't need a book, however groundbreaking, to tell us that, and Hart's little treatise was hardly groundbreaking, anyway. We've known that threat impairs cognitive processes since at least the 1930s, although a good Skinnerian would not use the phrase "cognitive processes." Mammals don't learn well when they're afraid.

Judy Willis, a neurologist, writes in her essay:

> ...choice, interest-driven investigation, collaboration, intrinsic motivation, and creative problem solving are associated with increased levels of such neurotransmitters as dopamine, as well

as the pleasurable state dopamine promotes. Novelty, surprise, and teaching that connects with students' past experiences and personal interests and that is low in threat and high in challenge are instructional strategies that appear to be correlated with increased information passage through the brain's information filters such as the amygdala and reticular activating system. (2008, p. 427)

So does that mean we should give kids injections of dopamine so that they'll be more creative? Notice the phrase "associated with" in the first sentence and "correlated with" in the second. We have correlations, not causal relations. Again, we don't need to know anything about the brain in order to teach any more than we need to know how internal combustion engines work in order to drive.

Dan Willingham of the University of Virginia puts it well when he underscores the chasm between neurons and the classroom:

So what has neuroscience done for us lately? Not much, because it's the classroom data that really matter. In principle, neuroscientists might suggest something that we could try in the classroom, and then we would decide—by behavioral (not neuroscientific) measures—whether it works or doesn't work. (2008, p. 423)

Probably no theory in recent years has captured the imagination of educators as much as Howard Gardner's exposition of multiple intelligences. I presume that they are well enough known that I won't spend a lot of time describing them in detail but merely summarize them (besides, for those unfamiliar with the concept, Gardner's initial exposition, *Frames of Mind* (1983), is a good read).

Gardner chastised schools for paying so much attention to two intelligences, linguistic and logico-mathematical. I don't know if he recanted his position at all, but in *The Unschooled Mind* (1991), he does note that these have served as the principle sources of mind development for the two major theorists of the 20th century, Jean Piaget (number) and Noam Chomsky (language).

But Gardner elevated five other abilities to similar status:

- **Spatial Intelligence**. "Central to spatial intelligence are the capacities to perceive the visual world accurately, to perform transformations and modifications upon one's initial perceptions, and to be able to re-create aspects of one's visual experience, even in the absence of relevant physical stimuli" (1983, p. 173).

- **Musical Intelligence**. This may be reflected in composing, playing instruments, singing, or some combination thereof. In Schopenhauer's words, as quoted by composer Igor Stravinsky, "the composer reveals the inmost essence of the world and utters the most profound vision in a language which his reason does not understand..." (in Gardner, 1983, p. 103).

- **Bodily-Kinesthetic Intelligence**. Bodily kinesthetic intelligence is seen in dancers, swimmers, instrumentalists (I could *know* a piece of music by heart and still hit the wrong key), many athletes, and a rare breed—mimes.

- **Intrapersonal Intelligence.** "The core capacity at work here is *access to one's own feeling life*—one's range of affects or emotions: the capacity to effect discriminations among these feelings..." (1983, p. 239).

- **Interpersonal Intelligence.** "The core capacity here is *the ability to notice and make distinctions among other individuals*" (1983, p. 239).

Gardner discusses the two personal intelligences together, but makes the case that they are ultimately separate.

Little empirical research lurks behind this delineation, and Gardner admits that establishing them was "reminiscent more of an artistic judgment than of a scientific assessment" (1983, p. 62). Gardner did establish criteria in order for a "talent" or "ability" to be known as an intelligence:

- Potential isolation by brain damage

- The existence of idiots, savants, prodigies, and other exceptional individuals

- A distinctive developmental history, along with a definable set of expert "end-of-state" performances

- An evolutionary history and evolutionary plausibility

- Support from experimental psychological tasks

- Support from psychometric findings

- Susceptibility to encoding in a symbol system (e.g., language, picturing) (1983, pp. 62-69)

Gardner has since added a "Naturalist Intelligence" that "enables human beings to recognize, categorize, and draw upon features of the environment" (Gardner, 1999). He has considered moral and spiritual intelligences, but to date, rejected them as perhaps pertaining to an existential intelligence. The jury is still out on that.

Some have called for the development of tests for the various new intelligences, something that Gardner has resisted, saying that you would need several tests of any one intelligence to get an adequate reading. After all, if you can express musical intelligence by playing an instrument, singing, or writing a composition, what one "test" would cover all the possibilities?

At the time he wrote his first treatment, *Frames of Mind*, in 1983, he had little or no interest in education applications of the theory. Although one chapter was indeed titled "Educating the Intelligences," its exposition was more about how different cultures affected them differently. When I asked him if he knew of anyone who was trying to make such applications, he rather sheepishly told me about a group of teachers in Indianapolis who hoped to establish a school based on the theory. He was pretty clear that he didn't think much would come of it. The evolution of the Key School is itself a bit of a fluke: three elementary teachers at one school were designated to develop a curriculum for gifted and talented students. They decided that Gardner's framework would make a useful frame for all students. The other teachers weren't having any of that, so the three rounded up five more who expressed interest and spent a year working nights and weekends developing a preK-6 program.

Gardner later became involved with and enthusiastic about what would be named the Key School, to the extent that he was asked to be a pallbearer on the untimely death of Pat Bolanos, the school's founder and principal. Others also took notice. In 1991, *NEA Today* put the Key School on its cover with the question, "Is this the best elementary school in the nation?"

It likely would have been a good school under any reasonable theory because of Bolanos, one of the few people I've known who could render big ideas into daily practice without trivializing them. This is not true of all those who have said they were practicing the multiple intelligences theory in their classrooms.

Why the popularity? Mindy Kornhaber answered that,

> ...the theory validates educators' everyday experience: students think and learn in many different ways. It also provides educators with a conceptual framework for organizing and reflecting on curriculum assessment and pedagogical practices. In turn, this reflection has led many educators to develop new approaches that might better meet the needs of the range of learners in their classrooms. (2001)

For me, whether or not Gardner's multiple intelligences theory accurately describes the brain and how it functions is not in the end all that crucial. Whatever its ultimate fate, one thing it does is indisputable: It throws a bright light on the dark, dreadful sterility of recent math-and-science obsessions emanating from policy makers and so-called reformers.

If Gardner's views seem too "far out," here is a more "traditionalist" statement:

> Social, emotional, and cognitive development are highly interrelated. Although each of these domains can be studied individually in a laboratory or described separately in its own chapter in a textbook, the brain is a highly integrated organ, and its multiple functions cannot be isolated from each other in vivo. (Shonkoff, 2006)

In vivo—in life as in the individual, in the family, in the community, in school.

In the same article, Shonkoff concludes,

> The challenge is clear, and the stakes are high. The number of children whose lives are threatened by social and economic adversity is unacceptably large, and the knowledge that could be used to promote their healthy development is exploding. The time has come to broaden and deepen the scientific foundations of developmental and behavioral pediatrics and to enlarge its field of active engagement. Central to this task is the need for stronger impact in the public policy arena that is grounded in science and avoids ideological advocacy. (2006)

No doubt Shonkoff would not have felt the need for that last sentence 6 years earlier.

Chapter 9:
The Goals of Public Education

In 1979, John Goodlad wrote *What Schools Are For.* New editions appeared in 1994 and 2006. Because Goodlad held the same position as when the 1979 version appeared, he only added new prefaces, plus an afterword to the 2006 edition. One chapter contains the 12 "Goals for Schooling in the United States."[14] The 12 goals listed were whittled down from over 1,200 Goodlad and his colleagues had gleaned from the statements of state and local boards and various commissions. Each goal has several more specific subgoals. I think it is advisable to read the entire list before rendering any kind of judgment or drawing any conclusions about the adequacy and/or appropriateness of the individual goals. Consciousness is indeed a stream, but often must be dealt with in segments sequentially. Some of the goals seem shortsighted until the later ones are also taken into account.

Goal #1: Mastery of Basic Skills or Fundamental Processes

- Develop the ability to acquire ideas through reading and listening.

- Develop the ability to communicate ideas through writing and speaking.

- Develop the ability to understand and utilize mathematical concepts.

---

14   The 12 "Goals for Schooling in the United States" are reprinted here with permission by the author, John Goodlad, and the publisher, Phi Delta Kappa International.

- Develop the ability to utilize available sources of information.
- Develop the ability to read, write, and handle basic arithmetical operations.

Commentary: Note that the *skill* of reading is last on the list and the ability to acquire ideas through reading is first.

Goal #2: Career Education-Vocational Education

- Develop the ability to select an occupation that will be personally satisfying and suitable to one's skills and interests.
- Develop salable skills and specialized knowledge that will prepare one to become economically independent.
- Develop attitudes and habits (such as pride in good workmanship) that will make the worker a productive participant in economic life.
- Develop positive attitudes towards work, including the necessity of making a living and an appreciation of the social value and dignity of work.

Commentary: This set I find troubling even as I recognize its salience to many people (Goodlad was uneasy about it, too). It seems more removed from the realities of the world than the others. I don't know if it's true, but I keep hearing that 90% of the jobs today's kindergartners will take don't exist yet. No one can know that for certain, but it's an indication of how rapidly some areas of the job world are changing.

Second, it assumes that the individual has control, that he or she "selects" an occupation. But there are things such as markets and laws of supply and demand that are not under the control of the individual. I came across a story recently about the difficulty in finding *any* job in parts of India. Getting a job depended on who you knew and social status more than anything else. When a position for subinspector at a police unit opened up, thousands of applications were received. Education, in and of itself, does not *create* jobs (University of Washington News, 2008).

Thirdly, it assumes that somewhere out there is a job that will yield satisfaction. Maybe not. I recall one instance of the comic strip Dilbert where Dilbert suggests that he and Wally start their own business. Wally says something like, "Why don't we keep our jobs and run the business from here?" Dilbert asks, "Wouldn't that be unethical?" And Wally replies "That only applies to people who are not already in hell." Back in the 1980s the number of people entering computer fields soared because that was where the money was. Later, but well before the dot.com bust, the numbers dwindled as people realized it took a certain *personality* as well as certain skills to actually enjoy jobs like writing code.

Fourth, a look at job projections from the Bureau of Labor Statistics (BLS) indicates that, while the proportion of jobs requiring a college degree will increase a little over the next decade, the overwhelming bulk of jobs will be in the low-level, low-pay service sectors. This is something the fearmongering critics cited early in this book never want to deal with. They only examine the supply side of creating skilled people, not the demand side. The authors of the book referred to by the University of Washington news release worry that having many educated people and few jobs could destabilize India.

But the critics would much rather utter clichés like "two-thirds of the 10 fastest growing jobs require a degree or some postsecondary instruction." "Some postsecondary instruction," of course, is a weasel phrase—who knows what it means? From a look at the BLS jobs projections, in most cases it means a high school diploma plus a few weeks to a few months of on-the-job training.

In addition, "the 10 fastest growing jobs" gives us a rate. Those 10 occupations don't account for many jobs. If I make one dollar today, two tomorrow and four the next day, my rate has doubled each day but all I have is enough money to eat at some fast food joint. According to the BLS, retail sales accounts for more jobs than the top 10 fastest growing jobs combined. Other low-skill, low-pay jobs like food worker and janitor or maid are right up there with retail sales. Next time you attend some professional conference, look around at the maids, busboys, waiters, etc., who make it all possible.

Fifth, given that jobs require specific skills, it is not realistic that schools can provide specific vocational training for many of them. Looking back, the most educatively salient moment in my son's life might have been when he was in seventh grade and I bought an Apple II computer (mostly for me, not him). He was a literature major in college, but now writes software that predicts when airplane engines with certain features will encounter problems and need to be serviced, repaired, or destroyed. Goodlad is aware of this too, and calls for more general experience. He points out that Dewey introduced woodworking into his school not to prepare future carpenters but to provide experience in a different medium of problem solving than what would be encountered from a book (sounds a bit like he might have had his own nascent theory of multiple intelligences).

Sixth, it seems to presume that schools should fit the child to society, not society to the child. Since these goals were written in the 1970s, they might reflect a reaction to the do-your-own-thing revels of the 1960s.

I would prefer the outside world of occupations be conveyed to children the way the Key School in Indianapolis did it.[15] They established a system whereby the faculty met every Wednesday after lunch for a planning and evaluation session. Parent volunteers would take kids to the auditorium-gym where someone from the community would explain what they did on their jobs. Once when I was there it was nurses and paramedics; another time a quartet from the Indianapolis symphony talked about their instruments and played, then took questions. The session was, in fact, a demonstration of how impoverished music is in most schools. In most schools, band begins for a limited number of students around fifth grade. In the Key School, everyone learns to play an instrument starting in first grade. During the Q & A, the quartet was obviously blown away by the sophistication of the questions.

---

15   At the time, the Key School was preK-6; it has expanded to include a middle and high school.

Goal #3: Intellectual Development

- Develop the ability to think rationally; that is, thinking and problem-solving skills, use of reasoning and the application of principles of logic, and skill in using different modes of inquiry.

- Develop the ability to use and evaluate knowledge; that is, critical and independent thinking that enables one to make judgments and decisions in a wide variety of life roles (for example, citizen, consumer, worker, etc.) as well as intellectual activities.

- Develop the ability to make use of knowledge sources utilizing technology to gain access to needed information.

- Develop positive attitudes toward intellectual activity, including intellectual curiosity and a desire for further learning.

Goal #4: Enculturation

- Develop insight into the values and characteristics of the civilization of which one is a member.

- Develop awareness of one's historical heritages—the literary, aesthetic, and scientific traditions of the past—and familiarity with the ideas that have inspired and influenced mankind

- Develop understanding of the manner in which heritages and traditions of the past are operative and influence the direction and values of society.

- Acquire and accept the norms, values, and standards of the groups of which one is a member.

- Examine the norms, values, standards, and traditions of the groups of which one is a member.

Commentary: I can't imagine a time when this list would not have seemed simple-minded. Maybe those who compiled the documents from which the list was derived were all or mostly White people. Living until recently in a school district with 105 languages spoken at home, the idea isn't even formable. It becomes more acceptable if we add "Apply this list to the other cultural groups that are part of your daily experience." Of course, there are an increasing number of people who are not only multiracial, but multicultural as well. The list becomes broadened in the next set of goals.

Goal #5: Interpersonal Relations

- Develop a knowledge of opposing value systems and their influence on the individual and society.

- Develop an understanding of how members of a family function under different family patterns.

- Develop skill in communicating effectively in groups.

- Develop the ability to identify with and advance the goals and concerns of others.

- Develop the ability to form productive and satisfying relations with others based on respect, trust, cooperation, consideration, and caring.

- Develop an understanding of the factors that affect social behavior.

Goodlad's own elaboration:

> Rapid personal and social change is taking place in today's society. Human beings are subjected to new and increasingly fragmented roles. In a complex, interdependent world, individual mental health is closely related to the large social structure—to one's interpersonal relations….Schools should help every child to understand, appreciate, and value persons belonging to social, cultural, and ethnic groups different from his own, and to increase affiliation and decrease alienation. (1979, p. 57)

Commentary: Looks like the world was already pretty flat in 1979. But too many children, suffering from "savage inequalities," will be impeded in developing these skills and abilities. Linda Perlstein spent over a year in a poverty-stricken school and wrote *Tested: One American School Struggles to Make the Grade*. She observes,

> It was once considered a given that a child's character was shaped at home and brought to school like a pencil box or a clean notebook. But just like today's children come without sharpened pencils, they often come without control of their emotions and impulses—a void that impedes academic potential more than any school supply. Many students also lack empathy. [The principal] told her teachers, "If you cannot connect with other people, you're never going to make decisions based on other people's self-interest." (2007, p. 66)

I wonder how much the findings about brain development and stress discussed in chapter 7 come into play here?

The first subgoal, of course, is precisely what fundamentalists of any religion do not want to happen in schools. Fundamentalist Christians do not want a course *about* the Bible. They want the Bible taught.

Goal #6: Autonomy

- Develop a positive attitude towards learning.
- Develop skill in selecting personal learning goals.
- Develop skill in coping with and accepting continuing change.
- Develop skill in making decisions with purpose.
- Develop the ability to plan and organize the environment in order to realize one's goals.
- Develop the willingness to accept responsibility for and consequences of one's own decisions.

> Schools that do not produce self-directed citizens have failed both society and the individual. *We have created a world in which there no longer is a common body of information that everyone must or can learn.* Schools should help every child to prepare for a world of rapid change and unforeseeable demands in which continuing education throughout his adult life should be a normal expectation. (Goodland, 1979, pp. 57-58, emphasis added)

Commentary: What must everyone know? Aside from being able to read in order to acquire knowledge (not just as a skill), arithmetic, oral communication, and, for Americans, American history and knowledge of life in a democracy, I can't think of anything.

I cannot offhand imagine anything dumber than the recent California mandate that all eighth-graders take algebra. One of three things will happen: a) algebra will get dumbed down, b) the dropout rate will increase, or c) both.

In a 2000 *Education Week* story, I cited an earlier *Washington Post* piece which described how parents "were rushing home from work, bolting down dinner, and going to school to learn...algebra. 'They came not for their benefit. They had learned algebra years ago and most of them had no use for X's and Y's in their current lives'" (Bracey, 2000a). This time they're doing it so they could help their *kids* get through algebra.

I am not alone in my judgment of California's folly. Many members of the National Mathematics Advisory Board agreed for one or both of the reasons given above. In addition, California will have to double the number of middle school algebra teachers. "It's a shortsighted policy that confuses taking a course with learning....It is absolutely far fetched," said Brookings Institution researcher, Tom Loveless (in Cavanagh, 2008).

The issue of who should take algebra and when is an old debate. It seems from what I've read that one large problem people seldom wish to talk about is how well it is taught. Often not well, I would guess. It's tough to generalize from an N of 1, but my daughter's algebra text was an endless series of unconnected procedures (ditto geometry). And then there's the classic from a NAEP assessment where students were told how many soldiers a bus would hold and asked how many buses would be needed to convey them from point A to point B. A plurality of students wrote "31 remainder

12." Videotapes of teachers teaching eighth-grade math in the U.S., Japan, and Germany found American teachers putting much more emphasis on procedures—how to do something—while German and Japanese teachers were more conceptually oriented (National Center for Education Statistics, 1999).

I take time to mention another outcome often quoted in accusations against schools in order to hopefully dismiss it. The problem goes, "There are 25 lambs and 5 goats on a boat. How old is the captain?" Most kids say 30. People take this to mean that American schools do not teach math sensibly. However, these results come to us from Switzerland—I do not believe they have ever been replicated in the U.S. and, even if they have, I don't think it shows that kids are dunces and teachers incompetent. Most adults, most of all, teachers, do not try to make fools out of children. If the teacher gives you a problem, surely it has a solution. We instruct the children to trust teachers. Twenty-five times 5 is too big and 25 divided by or minus 5 is too small so the answer must be 30.

Having said all of the above, I must emphasize that I am not making a case for ignorance. I am merely reflecting the third subgoal. The world is not only changing, it is an uncertain place. I took math through calculus. I occasionally make use of simple algebraic operations, but I haven't taken a derivative or found an integral since the final exam 48 years ago.

On the other hand, I took French in high school because that's what college-track kids did, and French in college because it was demanded by graduate school (that, too, was a stupid requirement. A lot of my peers wasted a quarter taking a foreign language course that left them unable to say more than "Bonjour," and not say it well at that). When and where I grew up, I scarcely expected to leave the state, much less the country. But then I did start to travel and French came in handy in not only France, but also Lebanon, Laos, and other countries. And then I did live for a while in Bordeaux at a time when French was not only useful but virtually essential.

The lesson I take from this is, given the uncertainties of life, you should learn as much as you can about anything that is offered because you can't know what's coming down the road. The Indian and Chinese kids observed in "2 Million Minutes" don't have to "worry" about such uncertainties. Their uncertainties involve only the odds against their attaining their goals. Indeed, they are so focused on their goals, I can only presume that they suffered severe disappointment when they didn't attain them.

Goal #7: Citizenship

- Develop a sense of historical perspective.

- Develop knowledge of the basic workings of the government.

- Develop a commitment to the values of liberty, government by consent of the governed, representational government, and responsibility for the welfare of all.

- Develop an attitude of inquiry in order to examine societal values.

- Develop the ability to think productively about the improvement of society.

- Develop skill in democratic action in large and small groups.

- Develop a willingness to participate in the political life of the nation and community.

- Develop a commitment to the fulfillment of humanitarian ideas everywhere.

- Develop a commitment to involve oneself in resolving social issues.

More than ever before, man is confronted with confusion regarding the nature of man's conflicting value systems; ambiguous, ethical, moral, and spiritual beliefs; and questions about his own role in society. There is a major struggle over the issue of whether man is for government or government is for man. (Goodlad, 1979 p. 59)

And this was in 1979.

Goal #8: Creativity and Aesthetic Perception

- Develop the ability to motivate oneself, to deal with new problems in original ways.

- Develop the ability to be sensitive to problems and tolerant of new ideas.

- Develop the ability to be flexible, to redefine skills, and to see an object from different points of view.

- Develop the ability to enjoy and be willing to experience the act of creation.

- Develop the ability to understand creative contributions of others and to evaluate them.

- Develop the ability to communicate through creative work in an active way (as a creator) or a perceptive way (as a consumer).

- Develop the commitment to enrich cultural and social life.

Goal #9: Self-Concept

- Develop the ability to search for meaning in one's activities.

- Develop the self-confidence needed for confronting one's self.

- Develop the ability to live with one's limitations and strengths.

- Develop both general knowledge and interest in other human beings as a means of knowing oneself.

- Develop an internal framework by which an individual can organize his concept of "self."

- Develop a knowledge of one's own body and a positive attitude toward one's own physical appearance.

Commentary: To me some of this seems dangerously close to navel gazing. And living with your limitations during the K-12 years sounds like it could degenerate into selling one's self short. As we shall see in the next chapter, in the section on taking responsibility, most school students are not in situations where they can discover either their limitations or strengths. The "guinea pigs," as they called themselves, had strengths they couldn't imagine they had until they were placed in a situation that forced them to take responsibility for what they learned next.

Combining 8 and 9 more generally seems to me to reflect a lot about the goals of the Eight-Year Study, discussed in chapter 10.

Goal #10: Emotional and Physical Well-Being

- Develop the willingness to receive new impressions and to expand affective sensitivity.

- Develop the competence and skills for continuous adjustment and emotional stability.

- Develop the ability to control or release the emotions according to one's values.

- Develop the ability to use leisure time effectively.

- Develop positive attitudes and habits towards health and physical fitness.

- Develop physical fitness and psychomotor skills.

Commentary: The use of leisure time is especially dear to my heart. According to a February, 2008 report, the American worker remains the most productive among the G7 nations (Office of National Statistics, 2008). This has long been the case, although it can change a bit if one factors work week length, work year length, and incarceration rates into the equation. Americans work longer each week and more days per year than in any other country and our incarceration rate is huge compared to the other nations, even worse than Russia.

It is when the American workers go home that they engage in less than edifying use of their leisure time. One needn't be a snob or an elitist to make such a claim. Flipping on the TV is sufficient proof.

Goal #11: Moral and Ethical Character

- Develop the judgment to evaluate events and phenomena as good and evil.

- Develop a commitment to truth and values.

- Develop the ability to utilize values in determining choices.

- Develop moral integrity.

- Develop an understanding of the necessity for moral conduct.

- Develop a desire to strengthen the moral fabric of society.

Commentary: These goals create a delicate path for teachers to walk as parents vary immensely in how much they think the school should be involved in character development.

I am of two minds about this list of goals. First, it is so much richer than the idiotic and impossible goal of having 100% of our students read at grade level. Second, it's devoid of the human qualities that allow us to come to terms with life. It says little about the personal qualities listed on page 4. It says nothing about the uncertainties of life mentioned on pages 175-178.

The list is much broader and more extensive than what I mostly read about in educational periodicals. Yet the reader of the list cannot help but notice that it contains the word "democracy" not at all and the word "democratic" but once. This is a severe short-coming and reflects a downward spiral of American education that was evident in 1979 and all the more so today.

How democratic can a school be when teachers operate from scripts that permit no variation, when principals sign contracts requiring X points of test gains each year as a condition of employment? Dewey was against it:

> The dictation, in theory at least, of the subject-matter to be taught, to the teacher who is to engage in the actual work of instruction, and frequently, under the name of close supervision, the attempt to determine the methods which are to be used in teaching, mean nothing more or less than the deliberate restriction of intelligence, the imprisoning of the spirit. (Dewey, in Kreisberg, 1992, p. 10)

For Dewey, schools in a democracy had to be democratic themselves and that meant a role for the teacher in what was taught and how. We can only imagine how he would react to a situation where administrators ordered teachers to operate from a script. "It feels like anyone could walk off the street and have my job" (Perlstein, 2007, p. 51). Some of us suspect that that is the point of scripts. De-professionalize teaching so any low-paid person can do it and, at the same time, turn children into passive workers and drones.

Dewey would have been more likely to approve of the above teacher's principal, who distributed a cartoon showing a teacher speaking to her class from the front of a roller coaster car, "Today we're going to learn about gravity." In fact, Dewey's stand on education and democracy produced his best-known quote: "Democracy must be reborn with each generation and education is its midwife" (Dewey, 1916, p. 22).

Goal #12: Self-Realization

- Develop an appreciation of the idea that there are many ways to be a good human being.

- Develop a better self.

- Contribute to the development of a better society.

Commentary: Again, this is a list that, while missing some key constructs, stands in stark contrast to the debased "conversation" about the nature of public schooling today.

Chapter 10:
The Lost Lessons of the Eight-Year Study

The Eight-Year Study is often represented and misrepresented in a number of ways. For one thing, it didn't last 8 years. It was more like 12 years. The 8 years in question are the 8 years between entering ninth-grade and attaining a bachelor's degree. Diane Ravitch dismissed it in less than a page as lacking generalizability (Ravitch, 2000, pp. 281-282). Patricia Graham doubted its conclusions but was more specific in her criticisms, noting that, given the Great Depression and the cost of higher education, students in the Eight-Year Study would have been a rather homogeneous, select group:

> These men [who conducted the study] believed, based on their own life experience, that doing well in school was nearly all that was needed to be a success, because that had been true for them. Such was not the case, of course, for women, for racial minorities, for Roman Catholics, Jews, for the majority of the U.S. population, all of whom were vastly underrepresented in the educational leadership of that era… Not surprisingly, family, home and culture were more important educationally than school by itself, a point that became increasingly clear to educational researchers in the second half of the twentieth century. (Graham, 2005, pp. 89-90)

Graham's comments do call attention to some limits of the study, but she and Ravitch both grossly mischaracterize it. In the first place, although the follow-up of the study looked at how well 1,475 students from the participating schools did in college, the focus of the study was on *all* students. If fact, the director of the study, Wilfrid Aikin, later wrote that he thought the results would have been even more dramatic had the project studied students who did not go to college. The organizers of the study realized that only 16% of high school graduates attended college, but the colleges dominated the structure of the high school curriculum for all students. The question was, what innovations would the schools develop if they were freed from the yoke of the universities?

Second, as will be clear as this exposition proceeds, the focus was not on "doing well in school." It was, or became, focused on student growth (following Dewey's conception of education as growth) and how to use that growth to sustain and improve democracy. A subgoal of that was to make schools themselves democratic institutions for students, teachers, and principals. That's a bit different from just "doing well in school." As described by Aikin (1942):

> Secondary education in the United States did not have a clear-cut, definite central purpose...Schools failed to give students a sincere appreciation of their heritage as American citizens... American youth left high school with diplomas but without insight into the great political, social, and economic problems of our nation.

Our secondary schools did not prepare adequately for the responsibilities of community life. Schools generally were excellent examples of autocratic, rather than democratic, organization and living...Not many (graduates) had developed any strong sense of social responsibility or deep concern for the common welfare.

The high school seldom challenged the student of first-rate ability to work up to the level of his intellectual powers. It was easy for him to "get his lessons," pass his courses. The result was that many a brilliant mind developed habits of laziness, carelessness superficiality [author's note: I would add cynicism]...The high school diploma meant only that the student had done whatever was necessary to accumulate the required number of units.

It is only after five pages of this litany of high school shortcomings that Aikin gets around to saying:

Finally, the relation of school and college was unsatisfactory to both institutions. In spite of the fact that formal education for five out of six of our youth ends at or before graduation from high school...what the college prescribed for admission determined, to a large extent, what all boys and girls of the United States could study in school. (1942)

The suggestion for the Eight-Year Study occurred at the 1930 meeting of the Progressive Education Association (PEA). Someone communicated the desirability for such a study to Wilfrid Aikin, then head of the John Burroughs School in St. Louis. Aikin never revealed who, but the idea was in the air. Over the previous years, members had complained that, while there were lots of progressive innovations in elementary schools, there were virtually none at the high school level. The 1930 conference focused on "College Entrance and the Secondary School." A few weeks after the conference, the PEA formed the Committee for the Relation of School and College with Aikin as chair. It invited 30 schools, more private than public, to participate and persuaded 300 colleges and universities to waive their usual entrance requirements for graduates of these schools.

The committee sought funding and initially received modest amounts from the Carnegie Foundation. In later years, it received more generous funds from the General Education Board, which allowed it to form new commissions to study emergent problems. There was a Commission on the Secondary School Curriculum and a Commission on Human Relations and, perhaps most important, an evaluation staff headed by Ralph Tyler. As students began to graduate from colleges, a Follow-Up Committee was formed to evaluate the outcomes.

Even if the schools were not representative of the nation as a whole, I think that there are many lessons in the Eight-Year Study that remain valid today, but have been mostly lost. My restatement of them appears in Figure 10.1, and explanatory text follows.

Figure 10.1. Restatement of Lessons From the Eight-Year Study

1. Like politics, all education is local. Forget state and federal mandates.

2. Education in this nation is, or should be, more about living in a democracy, than about academic achievement.

3. Testing should be a means of learning about individuals, not separating and sorting them.

4. Evaluation should lead to improved curriculum, instruction, and decision making, not to the punishment of teachers and administrators.

5. Teachers should teach students, not subjects, or, at the very least, not subjects alone.

6. Principals must be democratically oriented colleagues of teachers, not "bosses."

7. Students need to take some responsibility (being accountable) for what they learn (next), and enjoy doing it.

8. Scientifically based education is an oxymoron.
   (See next lesson).

9. Flexibility and a willingness to change course, to do something different, are critical to the educational process.

10. "When ends are taken for granted and means dominate educational discourse...teachers will rarely be in control of their work, and the reasons given for taking one or another course of action will become increasingly bureaucratic and unsatisfying" (Kridel & Bullough, 2007). This is widely known today as "defensive teaching."

1. Like politics, all education is local. Forget state and federal mandates.

Today, a lot is written about "best practices" and "scientific methods." At the time of this writing, some conservative activists advocate national standards and national tests. To the best of my knowledge, no one has shown them to be effective across the board. Finland, the top-scoring nation in PISA, has national standards, but teachers are encouraged to teach them in personal and idiosyncratic ways and to adapt them to the needs of their students.

The mammoth, eight-volume RAND study of federally instigated change, especially volume III, *The Process of Change*, found local efforts were the determining factor (Greenwood, Mann, & McLaughlin, 1975):

> Decisions about project continuation [once federal funds ceased] appeared to closely parallel (or could be predicted from) the decisions or motivations to initiate the project. Projects that were initiated with strong district support and which were also seen as a solution to a particular problem were incorporated almost without exception, albeit at varying levels. And without exception, those projects which represented an opportunistic response to available dollars and received little or no support from district administrators withered away, *even where project objectives were met*....(p. 50)

> An almost axiomatic lesson that emerged from our field experience was that people change more easily when the change helped them solve problems that are real to them. Projects that were expected to be incorporated into district practice were usually based on the staff's overriding sense of educational

necessity and the significance of the program and the proposed remedy. Our field experience implied that although categorical, targeted programs may be intrinsically more satisfying to the federal policy maker concerned about the national dimensions of a problem, it is unlikely that these programs will lead to much change unless the programs' aims fit local interest and priorities. (p. 51)

When McLaughlin revisited the study 10 years later, one of the conclusions that held up was "local conditions prevail."

While classrooms, schools, and school districts share common features—curriculum structures, grade structures, and student placement policies, as examples—they also differ in fundamental and consequential ways. A high school English course in a wealthy suburban classroom differs substantially from a course offered under the same title in an inner city school. The problems confronting California school administrators differ markedly from those faced by colleagues in Kansas. (1990, p. 13)

Earlier, Ralph Tyler, the person who oversaw the testing and evaluation component of the Eight-Year Study said, "Efforts to restructure [education] in general like the *A Nation at Risk* are absurd. You can't change a whole system that way; you have to begin with problems...identify particular problems and actually work with them as was the case with the Eight-Year Study" (in Kridel & Bullough, 2007, p. 11.)

The concept of local variation and changing course as needed was built into the foundation of the Eight-Year Study. Well, maybe "built-in" is not the best term; it happened by default. Wilfrid

Aikin, the chief chronicler of the study at the time, had this to say in a section of his book, *The Story of the Eight Year Study*, called, "The Schools Start in Many Different Directions":

> The proposals for their new work range over a wide field all the way from plans to teach "The Progress of Man through the Ages" to instruction in "Football from the Spectator's Point of View." Most of the plans were quite ambitious, stated in glowing, general terms. One school proposed to do these two things: "The school will present to its students the opportunity for fullest development as individuals, both in their formative years and in adult life; it further will contribute to the progress of society through increasing the value of their participation in present and future situations…Another school set for itself an even larger task: "Our program attempts to aid pupils to come to an understanding and appreciation of what civilization has meant from time to time in different cultures and continues to mean in terms of social organization, production and consumption, standards of living, order, individual liberty, group co-operation, ethical standards and achievements in the arts and literature" (Aikin, 1942). [16]

One can call them dreamers. So they were. But look what they thought *about* in contrast to the debased language and restricted scope of most educational reform since *A Nation at Risk*.

2. Education in this nation is, or should be, more about living in a democracy, than about academic achievement. and 6. Principals must be democratically oriented colleagues of teachers, not "bosses."

---

[16] Aikin's original book from Harper and Brothers is hard to come by. However, it has been put online jointly by the Maine Association for Middle Level Learning, the University of Maine at Farmington, and the Maine Center for Meaningful Engaged Learning. The new publishers have added some material, which appears in a different color. It is in an awkward format—one or two pages at a time, but it's good to have it around (www.8yearstudy.org).

The document at www.8yearstudy.org is formatted in such a way as to prevent a count of words in the whole work, but if it did, it is likely that the most frequent words would be democracy, democratic, and democratically. Domestically and abroad, things were looking pretty grim. It was not clear how or if the country could get out of the Great Depression and remain a democracy. Abroad, the growing appeal of fascism, with its glorification of youth, horrified PEA Commission members. The German Youth Movement gave new meaning to the social importance and political potential of adolescents. Eight-Year Study staff—most notably Bruno Bettleheim, Fritz Redl, Peter Blos, Erik Erikson, and Walter Langer—had fled Austria and Germany for refuge in the United States. They arrived with firsthand knowledge of the growing tensions in Europe. Many other PEA members were not hopeful about the future. America was at risk, and democracy was threatened as fewer young people found meaningful connections with the wider society (Kridel & Bullough, 2007, p. 35).

Aikin saw it this way:

> It is not enough to create better conditions for learning. It is equally necessary to determine what American youth most need to learn. Out of their searching study, the Thirty Schools came to realize that the primary purpose of education is to lead our young people to understand, to appreciate, and to live the kind of life for which we as a people have been striving throughout our history. Other things are important but only relatively so. It is necessary to teach the three "R's", science, language, history, mathematics, the arts, safety, vocations and most of the other subjects that now crowd the curriculums of the schools; but unless our young people catch the vision which has led us on through all generations, we perish. (1942)

Keeping the program oriented toward sustaining and improving democracy was a continuing effort. Four years into the study, the participating Denver schools realized that their curriculum insufficiently reflected the purposes of the program They then formulated a statement of philosophy:

> In formulating its philosophy, a school must determine its own beliefs concerning the nature of the individuals with whom it works and the character of the society which it serves. The Denver Public Schools regard human beings as dynamic and purposive, with a capacity for growth and the ability to develop through experience. The schools of Denver believe that a democratic society is the society most congenial to the optimum development of such individuals. Democracy, so conceived, is a way of life. This includes at all times (1) the free play of intelligence, (2) respect for the worth of individuals, that is placing human values first, and (3) the participation of all individuals in social living, which is broadly interpreted to include all human relationships.

> The chief function of the schools in a democracy is to conserve and improve the democratic way of life. (Aikin, 1942)

As for principals, Aikin observed,

> School administration in the United States has been autocratic, by and large, rather than democratic...The role of the democratic leader is more difficult than that of the benevolent autocrat. The school Heads found that it exacted patience and wisdom. Especially did it require faith in the intelligence and good will of teachers, pupils and parents...Tenure—security of livelihood—is not enough. The administrators in the participating schools saw that they must create conditions in which teachers dared to be honest in expressing their convictions. (1942)

It wasn't easy but democracy survived both fascism and communism and, according to Benjamin Barber, we became complacent. And some who would do away with the public schools made gains. Barber was incensed:

> If schools are the vessels of our future, they are also the workshops of our democracy. In attacking not just education, but public education, critics are attacking the very foundation of democratic civic culture. Public schools are not merely schools for the public, but schools in publicness; institutions where we learn what it means to be a public. (1995)

A few years later, Barber had become more concerned: "We have been nominally democratic for so long that we presume it is our natural condition rather than the product of persistent and tenacious responsibility. We have decoupled rights from civic responsibilities and severed citizenship from education on the false premise that citizens just happen" (1998, p. 220).

The people who framed the Eight-Year Study might have been dreamers but they were under no illusion that "citizens just happen," as evidenced by the Denver philosophical statement just cited.

Barber might be feeling better these days. It looks like the process of turning the Constitution into confetti has come to an end.

3. Testing should be a means of learning about individuals, not separating and sorting them. and 4. Evaluation should lead to improved curriculum, instruction, and decision making, not to the punishment of teachers and administrators.

Gresham's Law, bad money drives out good, is much older than Gresham's 16th century formalization of it. Aristophanes formulated something quite similar in 405 B.C. in *The Frogs* where he noted that, just as brass coins kept gold and silver out of circulation, bad politicians kept good ones out of circulation.

A variation on Gresham's Law appeared in Norman Frederiksen's 1981 book, *The Real Test Bias*, whittled down in 1984 to an *American Psychologist* article of the same name—bad tests drive out good. Frederiksen opens with a quote from a 1926 essay by A. Lawrence Lowell that appeared in *The Atlantic Monthly*. Lowell addressed the question of whether a student should study for grades (he called them "marks") or for knowledge. In part, Lowell said:

> If all examinations were conducted as to be an accurate and complete measure of the education the course is intended to give...then there would be no reason why the student should not work for marks, and good reason why he should. To chide a tennis player for training himself with a view to winning a match, instead of acquiring skill in the game, would be absurd because the two things are the same...if marks are not an adequate measure of what the course is intended to impart, then the examination is defective. If examinations were perfect the results would command universal respect and high grades would be a more general object of ambition. (Frederiksen, 1984, p. 193)

The question is, then, are standardized tests accurate and complete measures of the course? Or, in current terms, are they accurate and complete measures of standards set by states and districts? Frederiksen gave part of his answer in terms of the rise of testing and teaching to the test. This included reviewing studies that indicated "that testing increases retention of the material tested and that the effects are quite specific to what was tested." That is, there is no general or nonspecific transfer of learning.

He then turns to a question seldom asked: Does the format of the test matter? Many studies have answered this in the negative. As Frederiksen points out, though, "the evidence is based only on free-response forms that were adaptations of multiple-choice tests. Research that started with a free-response test and then adapted that to a multiple-choice test found very low correlations between the two formats" (Frederiksen, 1984). These free-response tests were of "ill-structured" problems—complex problems requiring the generation of ideas without definite criteria for when the problem is solved. "Most of the important problems one faces in real life are ill-structured, as are all the really important social, political, and scientific problems in the world today" (Frederiksen, 1984, p. 199). Indeed, at least part of the problem in curing the world's economic crisis is that it differs in many ways from the Great Depression—it is ill-structured and we've never been here before.

It would be unfair, though, to use such ill-structured problems in our standardized tests because schools do not teach students how to handle ill-structured problems. It is one desirable educational outcome—and only one of many—that is not tested and not taught. It exemplifies how the format of testing influences, if not outright determines, the format of teaching. "Accountability systems involving currently used tests are likely to improve the educational process only in the narrow sense that they perpetuate the teaching of what is measured and make it more effective" (Frederiksen, 1984, p. 199).

"Situational (ill-structured) tests are not widely used in testing programs because of considerations having to do with cost and efficiency" (Frederiksen, 1984, p. 200). Frederiksen closes with a story of personal experience. An assignment Frederiksen took on in World War II was to improve grading practices in Navy service schools. On arrival, he found that the best predictor of grades in gunnery mate classes was a reading comprehension test. He then noticed that teachers lectured based on manuals. He developed performance tests related to maintaining, adjusting, and repairing guns on a warship—a gunnery mate's real job. Teachers and students complained that the tests were too hard. But instructors started bringing more guns and had students practice maintaining and repairing them. Mechanical aptitude and mechanical knowledge became the best predictors of success in the school. You can change everything by changing the test: "The 'real test bias' in my title has to do with the influence of tests on teaching and learning. Efficient tests tend to drive out less efficient tests, leaving many important abilities untested—and untaught" (Frederiksen, 1984, p. 201).

Given the variation in the goals of the schools and the methods used to attain them, one might have expected that the Eight-Year Study would have dismissed out of hand any idea of a common test battery. It did not. The funders wanted it, and four organizations associated with the program were testing companies, including the Educational Records Bureau and the College Board (some of the delegates to a conference worried that a common testing program "would become as vicious as the College Board examinations") (Kridel & Bullough, 2007, p. 53). Usually, in any "partnership" between school people and university people, the academics dominate, and that occurred often with the Eight-Year Study, too. But in a 1934 conference, in what Kridel and Bullough call a "revolt," a group of principals rose up against the idea of any kind of common test battery. And won.

Which is not to say the project didn't develop tests. It constructed some 200 of them, but they were developed not by testing companies associated with the study, but under the evaluation staff headed by Ralph Tyler. Tyler insisted that teachers be intimately involved in all aspects of developing assessment instruments. Shortly after his appointment to head the evaluation team, Tyler spoke to the Third Educational Conference on Testing. He "called for new methods of collecting student data so that important educational purposes, thought to be intangible and incapable of assessment, could be appraised. He went on to argue that no one uniform evaluation should be implemented among the thirty schools" (Kridel & Bullough, 2007, pp. 75-76). He called his approach to evaluation "comprehensive appraisal" where instruments were designed to ascertain student development and not merely to determine the acquisition of knowledge and factual learning. For him, evaluation should begin with teachers discussing "what kinds of changes in its pupils the new educational program was expected to facilitate" (Kridel & Bullough, 2007).

Aikin indicates that tests, along with other parts of the project, were subject to experimentation and revision: "In the course of the seven years the Evaluation Staff devised about two hundred tests that were used experimentally, refined, and tried out again and again. Some of them were finally discarded as inadequate, but others have proved useful to the schools" (Aikin, 1942).

Aikin's descriptions of some of the tests are quite brief. Kridel and Bullough provide more elaborate discussion:

> Test 1.4, "Applications of Principles in Social Problems," addressed issues of race and class as well as economics and politics. In this test, students were asked to take a position on a specific problem or hypothetical situation pertaining to the use of a new invention (with economic implications), the graduated income tax, a high school graduation incident with racial overtones, and the tension between industrial profit and workers' health...Test 2.51, "Interpretation of Data," required students to determine whether evidence presented in test statements was sufficient to make a statement true, probably true, probably false, or false... Test 3.1, "An Interpretation of Literature," went much beyond a student's ability to summarize content. Students were asked not only to demonstrate their own understanding of a story but also to recognize another's point of view and to examine the narrative in relation to a philosophy of life and to human motives. (2007, pp. 82-83)

Where the tests concerned values, prompts embedded throughout tested the consistency of a student's beliefs, something teachers apparently found especially useful. Once teachers realized the tests went beyond factual knowledge, they began suggesting topics that would help them solve problems of their interest or concern. Tyler was sympathetic.

> Teachers' actual problems, not hypothetical situations, dominated his interests and guided the work of the staff: "Teachers have many such problems to solve, real problems, perplexing problems." Many of them can be partially if not wholly solved by means of similar investigations carried on by teachers themselves. (Kridel & Bullough, 2007, p. 86)

Although the Eight-Year Study embraced testing, it viewed testing as a means of divining information about what students needed next and it saw teachers as the touchstones of the test development.

I offer Kridel and Bullough's summary:

> When Tyler stood at the podium at the Third Annual Conference on Testing in the autumn of 1934, he could not have imagined a faithless time like ours—a time when teachers are seen by policy makers less as sources of solutions to pressing educational problems and more as impediments to improvements, a time when curricular creativity is conceived merely as replicating programs from site to site. (2007, p. 87)

5. Teachers should teach students, not subjects, or, at the very least, not subjects alone.

The cliché in this country is that elementary teachers teach students while secondary teachers teach subjects. The Eight-Year Study tried to break down that aspect of high school teaching.

> Through a series of planned experiences—all oriented toward fostering discourse, examining ideas, clarifying values, and attending to consequences—teachers and staff were able to come together and reimagine themselves and their work as educators, that is, good human beings maintaining faith that positive outcomes would result from conversation and community. Commission leaders learned that one of the most significant factors for improving schools was straightforward but profound: "When a group of teachers dealing with the same students begin to talk about human beings instead of subject matter, changes begin." (Kridel & Bullough, 2007, p. 196).

The leaders of the Eight-Year Study also decided that teachers needed to know more about the nature of their students in order to create meaningful learning experiences—specifically more about the nature of adolescence and adolescents. As noted above, the Great Depression had a profound effect on students and many educators felt they needed to do more to prepare students for an adult life in a more perplexing world. Noted, too, the Commission members were aghast at the role adolescents were playing in Germany, a role that caused the young to appear dangerous.

One commission group studied youth by case study methods, interviewing a cross-section of some 725 adolescents. Another developed a course on human relations from a conference attended by, among others, sociologist John Dollard, developmental psychologist Mary Fisher, family researchers Robert and Helen Lynd, and anthropologist Margaret Mead. The effect was to turn the teacher into a guidance counselor and some of the case study reports make the teachers sound more like psychiatrists and analysts than anything else. But the going philosophy was that guidance was an integral part of teaching. The philosophy was expressed succinctly by the staff of Tulsa High School:

> Pupil guidance is no longer a thing apart to be handled by an administrator. It is a definite part of the teaching activity—in fact—guidance has become the key to the learning situation. Group discussion of individual guidance problems is a challenge to each cooperating teacher to learn more about his or her pupils and their individual problems….The teacher is no longer the classroom drill master. He is most interested in the personal supervision and encouragement of pupil growth. The emphasis in the classroom is all on the pupil. (Moran, in Kridel & Bullough, 2007, p. 108)

7. Students need to take some responsibility (being accountable) for what they learn (next), and enjoy doing it.

The idea that schools should be democratic communities meant that students would need to end their usual roles as passive recipients of instruction. This shift in which the students would plan some of their course of study and develop curriculum stunned them.

> This was not how students and teachers were to behave. They reported that their new role "was difficult for us at first because we had always been told just what to do and when to do it. We were rather bewildered as to what the future held for us. Imagine us, telling teachers what we wanted to study!" (Class of 1938, in Kridel & Bullough, 2007, p. 153)

This new role was part of what was called "the core curriculum." "Core" meant something quite different in the Eight-Year Study than it does today. Today it connotes the individual elements that all students must study. For the Eight-Year Study it meant something closer to "interdisciplinary" or "multidisciplinary" or "project based." One group of 55 collectively wrote a book, *Were We Guinea Pigs?* when they were 17 and 18 years old. They reported that "all students in University School [a laboratory school at Ohio State University] are required to study science, social science, English, mathematics, and physical education." But the "core aspect of the program allowed them to plan some of their own studies. When they came to a new subject (such as communication), they divided into small groups to tackle separate topics, [sic] sent individual members out to hunt the answers to questions about the origin of human speech, the telephone, printing presses" (*Time*, 1938).

Of particular importance, it turned out, was a 2-year course called "The Nature of Proof."

> This course is intended to promote critical thinking, [sic] differs from the usual study of logic by being entirely practical. It is taught by shock-haired, Canadian-born Dr. Harold Pascoe Fawcett. Dr. Fawcett starts with an explanation of the principles of Euclidean geometry, goes on to show his students that every conclusion depends on assumptions and definitions and, when correct, follows a concise mathematical pattern. His pupils then analyze speeches, political platforms, advertising, riddle them full of holes. Not only did Dr. Fawcett's pupils rate higher than other high-school youngsters in tests on reasoning ability, but they got the best marks in the State in plane geometry. (*Time*, 1938)

The student-authors wrote to a national institute on propaganda and sought out the assistance of a psychology teacher (Kridel & Bullough, 2007, p. 154). However, cooperative teacher-pupil planning was not a means of letting teachers be a "guide on the side." "This did not mean that teachers abdicated their responsibilities and allowed pupils to pursue questionable topics, as critics have charged. Quite the contrary; teachers were expected to be more conscientious than they typically had been in traditional settings" (Kridel & Bullough, 2007, p. 155). By "conscientious," they meant that the teacher had to be on the lookout for possibilities, resources, and limitations that the students might not see on their own. It required a deep reservoir of knowledge of both subject matter and pedagogy.

It sounds a lot like my graduate school days.

That *Were We Guinea Pigs?* came to exist at all was a reflection of the Eight-Year Study in progress. The students' English teacher, Louise Labrandt, had to first convince the faculty and administration that the students could handle the task rather than the typical senior yearbook approach. Then she had to convince Holt Publishing that there was a market for such a book. In 1998, Northeastern Illinois University mathematics professor, Frederick Flener, tracked down and interviewed 21 of the 27 "guinea pigs" known to still be living. A number had obtained doctorates but remembered the course as the most powerful in their educational careers (Flener, 2001).

8. Scientifically based education is an oxymoron. and 9. Flexibility and a willingness to change course to do something different are critical to the educational process.

Here's why education can never be a science: education deals with sentient beings and each is different. Recall Haber's explanation for the popularity of multiple intelligences and Alan Roses' speech explaining that most drugs don't work on most people. In addition, scientific research, including educational research, deals with groups. In the simplest medical realm, there is a treatment group and a nontreatment group that usually receives a placebo. There cannot be a "nontreatment" group in educational research, only a group that continues to be treated as it was before. After the experiment, statistical tests determine if there is a significant difference between the two groups and the researchers might also calculate an "effect size."

If you look at the distribution of scores from a treatment and a control group after the treatment is over, you often notice that the variability of the experimental group increased. This means the treatment didn't work for everyone and, in some cases, it might have made things worse. This is, if the experiment compares Reading Approach A with Reading Approach B and there is a significant difference between A & B favoring B, it can still be the case that some kids who received Approach B are reading *worse* than when the experiment started.

But teachers don't deal with groups. They are in a more clinical situation (although one that often degenerates into dealing with the whole class). And they deal with a different group and set of individuals each year. Tyler knew this:

> Recognizing the value of formal, traditional research, he acknowledged that there would always be an important place for studies seeking to control variables and test hypotheses, yet he was convinced that such work was necessarily constrained...he understood that teachers work in specific classrooms and with individual children and that their primary concern is to ameliorate problems specific to this work and context. (Kridel & Bullough, 2007, pp. 86-87)

Kridel and Bullough (2007) refer to the Eight-Year Study as an *implementative* study.

> To understand the Eight-Year Study is to become familiar with a much different conception of school experimentation, one forgotten with the passing decades of "process-product" designs and federal incursion into educational policy making

and school practice. Eight-Year Study leaders pioneered a new approach to research: an *implementative study*, the first of its kinds in the United States. As such, it differed from the common "status study (a survey to document current practices), the "deliberative study" (a gathering of data to support normative recommendations for educational change), and the pilot-demonstration project, which so many assume the Eight-Year Study represented.

Implementative studies tested no formal hypotheses, upheld no specific models to be implemented and evaluated, and established no set of outcomes. Rather, the Thirty School Study [another name for the Eight-Year Study] embraced a robust and determined *faith* in experimentation as an "exploratory process" to include gathering, analyzing and interpreting data for the sole purpose of improving educational practice. (pp. 36-37)

So, was the study a success? I think the answer is an unequivocal and resounding "yes" and on many terms. Edward Knight reported that "The guinea pigs wrote more, talked more, took a livelier interest in politics and social problems, went to more dances, had more dates. Especially concerned with campus affairs were the graduates of the six most experimental schools. There were more dynamos than grinds among them" (1952, pp. 114-115). The follow-up staff reported 18 outcomes, 13 of which favored the "guinea pigs" and 5 of which showed no difference between the two groups (www.8yearstudy.org/5-6-110-112.html).

The graduates of the Thirty Schools:

1. Earned a slightly higher total grade average.

2. Earned higher grade averages in all subject fields except foreign language. [These differences ranged from small to miniscule except for mathematics, which was more substantial.]

3. Received slightly more academic honors in each year.

4. Were more often judged to possess a high degree of intellectual curiosity and drive.

5. Were more often judged to be precise, systematic, and objective in their thinking.

6. Were more often judged to have developed clear or well-formulated ideas concerning the meaning of education, specially [sic] in the first 2 years in college.

7. More often demonstrated a high degree of resourcefulness in meeting new situations.

8. Had about the same problems of adjustment as the comparison group, but approached their solution with greater effectiveness.

9. Participated more frequently, and more often enjoyed appreciative experience in the arts.

10. Participated more in all organized student groups except religious and "service" activities.

11. Earned in each college year a higher percentage of non-academic honors (officership in organizations, election to managerial societies, athletic insignia, leading roles in dramatic and musical presentations).

12. Had a somewhat better orientation toward the choice of a vocation.

13. Demonstrated a more active concern for what was going on in the world.

On some of the criteria, the progressives did not differ from those in more traditional schools.

1. Did not differ from the comparison group in the number of times they were placed on probation.

2. Did not differ from the comparison group in ability to plan their time effectively.

3. Did not differ from the comparison group in the quality of adjustment to their contemporaries.

4. Differed only slightly from the comparison group in the kinds of judgments about their schooling.

5. Specialized in the same academic fields as did the comparison students.

When students from the six schools judged to be the most experimental were compared to other progressively educated students
and students in the comparison group they "earned markedly
higher academic achievement rates" (stateuniversity.com, n.d.).

I am particularly taken with that active concern for what was going on in the world, but overall, consider the breadth of the criteria by which the study was judged. For Aiken the differences
added up to "This We Have Learned: Many Roads Lead to College Success" (Aikin, 1942). They certainly do not give any support to Ravitch's claim that "Progressive reformers believed that
the scientific movement in education had 'exploded' the theory of
mental discipline and demolished the rational for the academic
curriculum" (2000, p. 162).[17]

But the above are just the *student* outcomes. As stateuniversity.
com pointed out, "Important outcomes of the Eight-Year Study
included developing more sophisticated student tests and forms
of assessment; innovative adolescent study techniques; and novel
programs of curriculum design, instruction, teacher education,
and staff development" (Kridel, n.d.).

For Tyler himself:

> Among the most significant outcomes [of the Eight-Year Study]
> were...wide acceptance of the concept of educational evaluation

---

17   Ravitch's contention and, indeed, her whole book bring to mind a comment from her
      mentor, Lawrence Cremin, 40 years earlier: "There is currently afoot a simple story of
      the rise of progressive education, one that has fed mercilessly on the fears of anxious
      parents and the hostilities of suspicious conservatives. In it John Dewey...awakes one
      night with a new vision of the American school: the vision is progressive education.
      Over the years...he is able to foist the vision on an unsuspecting American people.
      The story usually ends with a plea for the exorcising of this devil from our midst and
      a return to the ways of the fathers. This kind of morality play has always been an
      influential brand of American political rhetoric, used by reformers and conservatives
      alike. But it should never be confused with history!" (1961, p. *viii*).

as a procedure for appraising the attainment of the several main objectives of an educational program. This concept largely superseded the narrower concept of testing in assessing educational programs and student progress...[and] The recognition by educational practitioners of the value of defining educational objectives in terms of the behavioral patterns students are encouraged to acquire. This process was shown to be helpful in defining objectives that could be used to direct curriculum planning, to guide instruction and to furnish specifications for evaluation. (1976, pp. 40-41)

Superseded the narrow concept of testing! Quick! Tell Washington and the state capitals.

10. "When ends are taken for granted and means dominate educational discourse...teachers will rarely be in control of their work, and the reasons given for taking one or another course of action will become increasingly bureaucratc and unsatisfying."

This is not actually a lesson from the Eight-Year Study, but a quote from Kridel and Bullough about our present state (2007, p. 134). The ellipsis omits the words, "as they currently do." It is hard to imagine a condition further removed from the Eight-Year Study—where principals' jobs are contingent on getting a specific increased score on a test each year; where teachers follow scripts; where the ends are totally prescribed and even the means are highly determined. While Dewey saw planning as necessarily short-term and where the actions that followed were contingent on the outcomes that preceded them, Susan Neuman saw NCLB as a means of stamping out creative teaching. No doubt she was not the lone NCLB representative to hold that view.

Chapter 11:
Democracy and Education

A lthough democracy is discussed often in chapter 9, I had planned to write an entire chapter with this title, the title of one of Dewey's more important books. But Richard Gibboney, Nel Noddings, and Deborah Meier have saved me the effort with their essays—a manifesto in Gibboney's case—in the September 2008 issue of *Phi Delta Kappan*. I could do no better; the essays are printed here; I believe you will enjoy them. The 30 schools in the Eight-Year Study might have been unrepresentative, but they were unrepresentative in the way that Jefferson, Washington, Franklin, Adams, and the rest of the Founding Fathers were un-representative—they still strove to embody universal ideas. The study started over three-quarters of a century ago, but it addressed issues that are at least as cogent now as then.

Why an Undemocratic Capitalism Has Brought Public Education to Its Knees: A MANIFESTO*

By Richard A. Gibboney

Richard A. Gibboney is a former elementary teacher at the Andrew Jackson School in Ferndale, Michigan. He also is a former Pennsylvania deputy secretary of education for research and development and the former Vermont commissioner of education. He is the recipient of the Lindback Award for Distinguished Teaching, Graduate School of Education, University of Pennsylvania, Philadelphia.

* Permission to reprint granted by the author, Richard A. Gibboney, and the publisher, Phi Delta Kappa International.

Unchecked capitalism is destroying our nation's public schools, and No Child Left Behind (NCLB) is the final nail in their coffin. Marching under the banner of "accountability," right-wing, pro-business forces are willfully undermining the democratic right of all children to a free, high-quality education.

Rather than support policies designed to reduce poverty and its toxic effects on the ability of children to succeed in school, our lawmakers are pursuing the misbegotten path of penalizing schools in poverty-stricken cities and rural areas for their failure to work educational miracles. In so doing, they are eroding the promise of our democracy.

Most children at the bottom of the economic ladder start their formal education years behind middle-class children in language development, social behavior, and general knowledge of the world. This self-evident fact, repeatedly confirmed in research studies, creates a learning gap of Grand Canyon proportions between the children of social privilege and those who grow up poor, who are disproportionately black and Hispanic.

No system of schools—public or private—has ever demonstrated that it can close this poverty-induced learning gap for most children. If policy makers know this—and they surely must—they ignore it. In fact, in the two decades preceding No Child Left Behind, a succession of presidents and Congresses gradually abandoned historically successful Great Society programs that had lifted many of the poor out of poverty. Today, more than one-quarter of American children live in poverty, more than in any other industrialized nation.[1]

At the same time, those in the corporate elite and their political allies have ratcheted up the pressure on schools with a harsh accountability system that they have consistently shunned for themselves. Can you imagine applying to Enron and the Wall Street financial manipulators who brought us the credit and home foreclosure crises the same punitive standards we now apply to the schools?

> *No Child Left Behind has made public education itself fair game for profiteers, and this can only mean two things: corruption and higher costs.*

With No Child Left Behind, Congress ratified an upside-down education reform strategy: improve learning by feeding children less and testing them more. For those schools most affected by the false standards of NCLB—largely the ones in our poorest neighborhoods—all creativity, intelligence, and imagination have been sucked out of teaching and learning. The premise of the law—holding schools accountable for test results without any guarantees that students have received expert instruction in safe, well-equipped schools—contravenes science, flouts morality, and makes no economic sense.

And in what I believe to be a historic and an unconscionable failure, our nation's educators have stood by and let all this happen. Instead of relying on the energizing principles of democracy—equity, opportunity, and fairness—to fight this law and the mindset it grows out of, educators have taken political and professional cover in technicalities.

Teacher unions and groups representing administrators and superintendents have protested No Child Left Behind only around the edges and primarily from a narrow and self-interested intellectual point of view. They have not engaged in meaningful policy debates about the relationship of poverty to educational achievement, the essential role public education plays in our democracy, the huge disparity in wealth between the "haves" and the "have-nots," or the role of schools in creating citizens/workers who can think. We educators cannot continue to act so thoughtlessly, or this nation will not survive as a democracy.

I am not saying, as knee-jerk critics of my viewpoint allege, that poor children cannot learn. Neither teachers nor policy makers should be allowed to hide behind this facile and insidious assumption. This Manifesto is not about the so-called soft bigotry of low expectations that denies poor children a path out of poverty.

Given all that we know from neuroscience about early brain development and the role of environment in nurturing aptitude, schools cannot be expected on their own to close the achievement gap between rich and poor. Yet teachers are pilloried and innocent children intellectually abused for failing to learn under the drill-for-skill, test-'em-often methods advocated by the Bush Administration, by both political parties, and by the biggest lobbying group in Washington, the U.S. Chamber of Commerce.[2] The leadership of the nation and of public education seems not to understand that an undemocratic capitalism wants to destroy public education in favor of a system of private and for-profit schools paid for with taxpayer money.

NCLB THREATENS PUBLIC SCHOOLS

No Child Left Behind has made public education itself fair game for profiteers, and this can only mean two things: corruption and higher costs. This law turns over huge chunks of public education to those whose overriding goal is to make money, not educate children. Note the questionable tutoring industry that has materialized to provide "supplemental services" without solid evidence to date that it has helped poor children. And according to Jonathan Kozol, the test-prep and testing industry generated $2.8 billion in 2005.[3]

But those whose jobs are most threatened by the destruction of the public education system—teachers and administrators—have been unwilling to grasp the import of these developments. Their reaction confirms my thesis that our democracy is "tied and bound." Educators, too, are intellectual captives of the radical, un-democratic capitalism that has taken over our nation.

UNIONS ABANDON THE FIGHT

The best that the National Education Association has mustered in response to NCLB is the shrill complaint that Congress has declined to "fully fund" this disastrous law. The feeble response of the NEA is a sorry comedown for an organization that was once a vigorous defender of public education.

In *Whose America? Culture Wars in the Public Schools*, education historian Jonathan Zimmerman outlines how the radical Right in the 1940s and 1950s attacked public schools on several fronts:

communism, internationalism (the United Nations), and "sexual depravity"(which it linked to race). Back then, however, these fearmongers had to face down an NEA that knew how to beat them at their own game.

In 1941, to counteract assaults on social studies textbooks, the NEA established the National Commission for the Defense of Democracy Through Education. In 1949, it teamed with the Rockefeller Foundation and the Carnegie Corporation to form the National Citizens Commission for the Public Schools, a body that included such distinguished citizens as Roy Larsen, president of Time, Inc. Both commissions used multimedia and advertisements to counter right-wing attacks.[4]

This advocacy touched me personally. When I was a teacher in a progressive school system in Ferndale, Michigan, during the height of Sen. Joseph McCarthy's Red-baiting, our staff was attacked by Allen Zoll. I remember his name as if it were yesterday. Zoll, the leader of a national right-wing organization with fascist connections, was an anti-Semite and a hater of public schools. His innuendo-ridden pamphlet was cleverly titled *How Red Is the Little Red School House?* The NEA was not timid then about using forceful public relations strategies to lash back at Zoll on behalf of both our district and public education in general.

But times have changed. Today, the NEA is quiet and is not engaged in defending public education directly through citizen involvement and headline-grabbing commissions, as it once did. Its blind acceptance of NCLB is akin to an innocent man's complaint on the way to the gallows that the hangman bought too cheap a rope.

Randi Weingarten, president of the American Federation of Teachers, also buys into what I call the child- and teacher-destructive essence of NCLB. In the October 2007 edition of her advertorial "What Matters Most," in the *New York Times*, Weingarten calls for changes to the test-based accountability system, not for its elimination. Like her colleagues at NEA, she prefers to ignore the role poverty plays in low student achievement and shows that she implicitly believes New York City schools can close the achievement gap between socially privileged students and those who are less privileged. This is nonsense.

Weingarten prefers to ignore data indicating that children in some of our most poverty-burdened schools post achievement test scores on a par with those of some Third World countries. In 2003, students in Washington, D.C., for instance, scored lower than those in 36 nations in mathematics, and 26 nations outscored Mississippi students in science.

TABLE 1. Eighth-Grade TIMSS Science and Math Scores by Degree of Poverty School Attended		
	Score	
Poverty Level	Science	Math
Wealthy Communities	571	547
High-Poverty Communities	461	444
U.S. Average	527	504
International Average	473	466
Source: Data from Third International Mathematics and Science Study, 2003. Adapted from David C. Berliner, "Our Impoverished View of Educational Reform," *Teachers College Record*, August 2005, Table 2, p. 17.		

But when one looks at average state scores in the 14 states where there is no massive urban poverty, we find that only one nation, Singapore, scored above those states in science.[5] Even if they teach test-prep and retest, NCLB-style, 35 hours a week, teachers and schools by themselves cannot reverse the crushing effects of poverty and unstable families on educational potential.

Notice in Table 1 that both science and mathematics have a similar pattern: students in wealthy communities score about 100 points higher than students in high-poverty communities. Our socially privileged students are also nearly 100 points above the international average. This does not look like a failing school system to me. There is a huge political and democratic failure, however, in our toleration of poverty, but those among the elite don't want to talk about it. It's a safer "wealth protector" to deflect public attention to our "failing" public schools and to ignore the poor.

School superintendents are also misguided. As for school administrators, they are busy gaming the system by manipulating test-score results and subgroup sizes to make their schools look better rather than condemning NCLB itself as an attack on the oldest, most democratic system of public education in the world. In January 2004, I sent to 225 randomly chosen Pennsylvania superintendents (out of 501) a five-page abstract of "No Child Left Behind: Reform or Trojan Horse?"—an unpublished paper I had written. A short handwritten note from me invited their reaction. I received but 10 responses. One interested superintendent invited me to a discussion on NCLB with about 20 of his colleagues. That was it.

Even Phi Delta Kappa has succumbed. In 2006, its advocacy committee endorsed reauthorizing the law with amendments designed to "make it better." I hate to say it, but I think that, within the education profession today, numbers (i.e., test scores) are revered while ideas are suspect. The leadership of the teacher unions and the education professoriate are lost in a deceptively appealing array of disciplinary techniques typically devoid of democratic, theoretical, and historical content and, therefore, without practical democratic effect.

The superintendents and the PDK advocacy committee are examples of one reason why societies fail, according to Jared Diamond in his brilliant book, *Collapse*. That is, the leadership fails to identify a threat to society even though the cultural knowledge at the time is sufficient to recognize the threat. What the superintendents and PDK failed to see is that education is an idea game, not a technique game.[6]

DEWEY ABANDONED

As the practitioners and professors wander in this disciplinary thicket, they abandon the humanistic and generous philosophy of John Dewey. Dewey saw the sharing of ordinary experiences and interests as something to value; he described democracy as life lived (not just talked about) in a community "of varied and shared interests." Dewey feared, however, that without an intelligent vigilance, the few would take over from the many, the rich would dominate the poor, and the common good would be replaced by plutocratic corporate private interest.

> *Dewey feared that without an intelligent vigilance, the few would take over from the many, the rich would dominate the poor, and the common good would be replaced by plutocratic corporate private interest.*

Sadly, Dewey's fears are being realized. I can only conclude that educators have been seduced by the viewpoint that considers only the economic value of schooling as a training ground for workers and not the centrality of public education to the survival of democracy. In the endless parade of education "reforms," a focus on technical skills has replaced the pursuit of ideas, democratic ideals, and civic courage. My 1994 book, *The Stone Trumpet*, analyzed 34 reforms put forth by governments, foundations, researchers, and educators between 1960 and 1990. Only six fully cultivated democratic and intellectual values.[7]

By treating NCLB only as a technical and political problem rather than as a grave threat to democracy and to public education, our anti-intellectual unions and timid leaders undermine democracy itself. You may think that I am overstating the case. But all U.S. presidents, beginning with Ronald Reagan, along with a succession of Congresses, have favored the interests of corporations over the democratic and economic concerns of citizens. This pro-business bias has been hostile not just to public education, but to other social goods, including progressive tax policies and universal health care.

Structural changes in the economy—summarized in the term "globalization"—have opened new investment opportunities and sources of profit for such companies as Wal-Mart and have induced new stresses for their employees who work for "low pay and elusive benefits," as Robert Reich puts it.[8] Other economists such as James K. Galbraith, Paul Krugman, and Joseph Stiglitz acknowledge this fact as well.

Reich says that by 2007 corporations and wealthy individuals owned both the Democratic and Republican parties and the U.S. Congress. He outlines the threat to democracy posed by a voracious capitalism (although I don't think he discusses sufficiently the threat to our basic institutions, including public basic and higher education). While real wages for most workers have barely grown since the mid-1970s, executive compensation has soared to obscene levels, even for corporate leaders who have run their companies into the ground and brought disaster to our economy.

As a result of the administrations of the first President Bush and of President Clinton (who directed one of the most pro-business Democratic administrations ever), and in response to the destructive policies of the current President Bush, the undemocratic capitalist fox has been steadily devouring the public chickens. Medicare, Social Security, and any chance for widespread, publicly supported early childhood education have all been imperiled.

DEMOCRACY IN JEOPARDY

Next to go will be democracy itself. Think about it: What democratic civilization has ever thrived on the curious notion that its proper goal is making widgets for 50 cents and selling them for 100 cents regardless of the human, environmental, and social cost? Can such thinking ever lead to justice and domestic tranquility?

This obsession with profit-at-any-social-cost is inherent to capitalist philosophy. But most Americans are ill informed in this area or refuse to believe that the ax will ever fall on them.

Economist Duncan Foley, in *Adam's Fallacy: A Guide to Economic Theology*, explains how capitalism is good at doing some things well, like money accumulation for capital investment. On the other hand, he says, capitalism creates income inequality, tolerates poverty, and is hostile to the physical and democratic environment—including public schools. Foley speaks directly to my vision of "democracy tied and bound." He writes: "[Capitalism] creates new sources of wealth *and ways of life by destroying existing sources of wealth and community*" (emphasis added).[9]

> *The guardians of democracy—the leaders of our government and public institutions—have not been zealous in pursuing democratic goals.*

Do not lightly pass over the italicized words in the preceding paragraph. You have just read the most socially radical words in the economic lexicon. Blue collar workers in Ohio and Pennsylvania may not know the words "[capitalism] destroys existing sources of wealth and community," but they feel the slashes an abstract economic idea can inflict.

But you will not find Foley's ideas in the incessant stock market reports and business commentary on TV, on radio, or in print. In these media, capitalism is implicitly characterized as a gift-giving Santa Claus, world without end. Few if any of the high social costs of unfettered capitalism get in the way of the 24/7 Good News.

At the same time, I've come to understand that the captivity of democracy by market forces is not the result of a corporate conspiracy. On the contrary, corporations are doing what they are "wired" to do: work fiercely for competitive advantage regardless of social or environmental considerations. Reich points out that "Wal-Mart executives are only doing what they are supposed to do: Make money for their investors and give customers low prices. Like players in any game, [Wal-Mart] executives are doing *whatever is necessary to win*" (emphasis added).[10]

We have gotten into the mess we're in today because the guardians of democracy—the leaders of our government and public institutions—have not been equally zealous in pursuing democratic goals. Instead, they have let themselves be seduced by the worst of capitalism's lures.

CAPITALISM NOT SOCIALLY NEUTRAL

Capitalism is never socially neutral; its effects ripple deep and broad. Take the development of the automobile and its radical effects on community life as a provocative example of technology's powerful influence on daily life in our democracy. In the short term, the auto industry made its creators and manufacturers rich and created a whole new market. But cars also made the suburbs possible, drained talent and money from cities, and stimulated massive highway building, which helped to create today's sprawl. At the same time, the automobile industry offered high-paid, if routinized, work that helped build the middle class after 1950. Today, automobiles contribute to global climate change, to our dependence on oil, and, it has been argued, to our ongoing engagement in Iraq.

Anyone who acts as if capitalism is socially neutral is not looking at the real world. The beast feeds itself by using its raw power to prosper. Our failure to hang onto our democratic ideals has permitted the social good brought on by innovation to morph into orgies of overindulgence by the privileged few.

And you know how this will always pan out. While families with incomes in the top 20% own about 90% of the nation's wealth, 80% of American households live on less than 10% of that wealth. It is clear that poor and working-class families are not receiving their fair share of the wealth they have helped to create by being good citizens, by working, and by raising their children.

From 1983 to 1998, the household gain in wealth for the bottom 80% of U.S. households—that is, most of us—was a mere 9%. For the next 19% of households, the figure was more than four times as much, 38%. What about the top 1%, you ask? Their wealth increased by a whopping 53%.[11] Such data make plain why schools alone, since school achievement is tied so closely to social class, will never be able to close the rich/poor, white/minority achievement gaps. But if we look at the net worth of white and black families in America, we can see in simple numbers the huge disparity of wealth that reduces the achievement of poor minority and white youth in public schools, because school achievement is related to social class and class is related to wealth. Median net worth in 2004 for black families was less than $12,000; for white families, about $118,000.[12] These figures are less than democracy demands. Even the white family figure is low because it would pay for about three one-week hospital stays for a serious illness.

NCLB UNDERMINES PUBLIC TRUST IN SCHOOLS

Facts about inequality haven't stopped the corporate elite that brought about this huge imbalance in wealth from blaming the public schools for the very low achievement of poverty's children. In No Child Left Behind, the full power of the federal government was mustered to implement a law that undermines the public's trust in education, needlessly requires the involvement of private corporations in the work of public schools, and imposes unscientific standards, punitive sanctions, and impossible deadlines for "results." All of this virtually ensures the failure of most schools with high proportions of poor and minority students, while harassing teachers and students with needless and expensive testing.

For many critics, teachers have become the villains in the wealthy elite's panic over educational accomplishment and foreign competition. But teachers don't cause financial meltdowns, home foreclosures, climate change, or hurricanes. And they don't invade countries or outsource jobs. Teachers don't cause mind-numbing conditions of poverty that limit children's ability to learn. However, teachers are the ones asked to cope with the poisonous effects of poverty. Why? Because most of society doesn't give a damn.

With our nation's demographics rapidly changing—black and Hispanic students now make up 42% of public school enrollment[13]—and the historically persistent correlation between minority status, poverty, and low achievement, one can imagine the results for public schools when the media give their usual shallow treatment to the predictably low achievement of these blameless children. More and more public schools will be dishonestly labeled "failures," and our democracy will be weakened and further imperiled.

> *Many psychological and sociological studies are useful, but they have not created a robust theory of education.*

Harvard sociologist Orlando Patterson begs us to understand and acknowledge our own history, recounting the "familial ethnocide" inflicted on African Americans by Southern slaveholders. In most cases, the post-slavery descendants of slaves have yet to recover fully from this assault on the black family. The result, Patterson writes, has been a lack of parental support and discipline, the absence of fathers from the lives of 70% of black children born to single mothers, and the recourse of young people to gangs as parental substitutes. "By whatever means . . . lower class Afro-Americans have got to recommit themselves. . . to stable [families] . . . and to raising their children," he writes.[14]

This bit of social science research reveals the false premises of NCLB and the absurdity of educators who did not apply the data of their ordinary school experience to understanding the law's hypocrisy. Until our supercapitalistic democracy recognizes the rights of the poor and moves to correct this shameful legacy, children, disproportionately black and increasingly Hispanic, will be needlessly denied the privileges of middle-class family membership, which motivates them to learn and to do well in school. Unless more families are helped to grow into the working and middle classes over several generations, their children will continue to achieve at Third World levels in New York, Philadelphia, Detroit, and Washington, D.C. And no fast-talking superintendent of schools—or even a CEO of schools—will make any difference for most children in poverty-stricken families.

In this presidential election year, only former Sen. John Edwards spoke directly to the issues of poverty and class. Overlooking such an elephant in the living room is a measure of political neglect beyond reason. One would hope that our political leaders would act as if they understood that extreme inequality of wealth and child poverty are detrimental to a vital democracy.

TWO FACES OF POVERTY

Before I go into my recommendations, let me try to put two faces on the seemingly unreal problem of child poverty and the unbelievable amount of learning and positive attitudes that socially privileged children acquire at home and bring to school. First, take my young friend Gabriella. Gabriella lives along Philadelphia's Main Line, a 30-mile stretch of affluent suburbs running along the old "main line" of the Pennsylvania Railroad.

To know Gabriella is to know how a rich and informal home learning environment can lead to phenomenal language and cultural learning by age 10. Her parents believe that the "cultivation of the mind and feelings is the best life and the best preparation for life" (interview with Gabriella's mother). Gabriella started improvising songs and dances with her mother when she was just 2, attended a high-quality preschool, has 300 books in her home, reads or is read to every night, has traveled to Italy and Hong Kong, regularly visits museums, and has attended Broadway shows. When she studied the Colonial period in school, Gabriella dressed herself and her dolls in Colonial clothes, and her parents helped her get library books on Colonial crafts and cooking. Her love of learning was fostered at home; her well-endowed school system can now build on her already solid knowledge and drive to learn.

Then consider Anthony, a young man I don't know personally, who lives in Newark, New Jersey. Anthony was abandoned as a toddler by his crack-addicted parents and grew up in a succession of unhappy foster homes. He was finally taken in by a hospital housekeeper who was a distant relative. But Anthony ran away when he thought he was being asked to do too many chores and now lives with an aunt. Once, he had a penchant for shoplifting, and he still tends to settle any disputes with his fist, a habit he is gradually breaking under the mentorship of Newark's mayor, Cory Booker, who took Anthony and two other boys under his wing.

Under No Child Left Behind, the same tests are administered to Gabriella and Anthony, and the same results expected. Their family lives and their school lives are in stark contrast. Gabriella's family is nurturing, and her school intellectually enriching. Anthony's family is dysfunctional, and his school overburdened.

Does this make any sense? No wonder our democracy is tied and bound.

THE DOXOLOGY

The sun stands low on the democratic horizon. Where are the leaders we need? Who or what will break the eerie silence? With more than three million teachers and education professors, with two powerful unions, with enormous potential to raise many millions for a nationwide fight in the media against an adversary we've known since the 1950s, why have we chosen to play dead?

Isn't fighting for public education and democracy the worthiest of causes? How can you not join an army where no one is killed and everyone wins? Our enemies fight a ruthless fight, and if they win, everyone loses. Lies unchallenged are lies believed. Just ask John Kerry.

An enemy with a clear and firmly held set of beliefs, however destructive and unjust, has to love having wimpy opponents like us. We wilt at a frown. What, for God's sake, are we so afraid of? With leadership like this, World War II would have been a walkover for the Axis. Why do we line the darkening streets, silent before the march of the economic authoritarians?

Today, the voices of protest are weak and scattered. In the ordinariness of defeat, this day appears as any other in a century of days, and the ordinariness of this day mutes any instinct to cry out at the loss.

Why the silence? No one told the people. Sixty years of successful attacks have left public educators so addled that our leaders accept the corrupting ideas and values of those who would destroy us. We have adopted their false language of accountability, standards, profit, privatization, competition, and numbers. We then suffer the punitive and harsh demands of NCLB, the weapon designed to destroy us, inch by test score inch.

The "achievement gap" between the privileged and the poor will endure until the elite discard their damning "bigotry of low social expectations," expectations that have imprisoned generations in poverty and closed the door to their entry to the middle class.

Another decade of attacks in a procorporate federal administration of whatever party, and public education will be two heartbeats from death. The poor and the working class will suffer grievously.

Democracy is a verb, not a noun for a dead category.

RECOMMENDATIONS

1. ADDRESS THE PROBLEMS OF POVERTY AND CAPITALISM

If we as a society ever muster the courage to enact the two recommendations I am about to offer for dealing with the problems created by poverty, we are certain to close the achievement gap between socially privileged students, who are mostly white, and less socially privileged students, regardless of their ethnicity or color.

- *Long term.* Begin a systematic plan to bring at least half of the families living in poverty into the middle class in a generation. That is, by 2033. Bring the other half of families into the middle class by 2058.

- *Short term*. Establish excellent public prekindergarten programs for all 3- and 4-year-olds.

There is reason to believe we can reach all of these goals. Prekindergarten programs were part of Prime Minister Tony Blair's 1999 pledge "to end child poverty forever." By 2006, 700,000 kids—17%—were lifted out of poverty and found themselves within shouting range of Blair's short-term goal.[15]

Known as Sure Start, Britain's program looks a bit like a 1960s community action program in the U.S. But the British one is community action on steroids. The school becomes a center in which all social services combine to help the poor, working parents, and children of the middle class. A reporter for the *Guardian* describes the school/social centers this way:

> Every child from birth finds here everything necessary to thrive, especially for those who never see a book at home or learn to count, and barely talk. Here speech therapists, social workers, [home] health visitors, and high-calibre nursery teachers help all children reach primary school ready to learn. Here working mothers are guaranteed affordable child care, in a place where parents of all [social] classes create a hub for the local community. That's the dream and in some places it's all there.[16]

The U.S. has tackled major social problems before. In 1935, Congress created Social Security. At the time, older people were the largest poverty group in America. In about 65 years—slow and steady—90% of this group had climbed out of poverty. Today, children are the biggest poverty group in America.

Nobel prize-winning economist Joseph Stiglitz, in *The Roaring Nineties*, argues that the nation can afford to address poverty directly. "We could, if we wished," he writes, "end domestic poverty and malnutrition. We could, if we wished, ensure that everyone had a basic modicum of health care. . . . The United States chooses not to provide these basic services, because it chooses not to tax itself."[17]

Implementing my recommendations—moving poverty families to the working class and middle class in two generations and establishing excellent early childhood programs for all social classes—will truly leave no child behind. If we act on these two recommendations, the achievement level of public school students will slowly rise. Moreover, our national obsession with premature quantitative evaluations of new programs—a major error that Britain avoids—kills potentially successful programs before they can show their *social/democratic* worth.

2. DEVELOP A COMPREHENSIVE AND DEMOCRATIC THEORY OF EDUCATION

We have lost our *idea* of the democratic purpose of public education, and that has infected our practice and policy making. NCLB is my evidence. We badly need to restore a comprehensive theory to undergird our policies. I believe John Dewey's theory of education is our best choice.

Dewey's theory of education is the only extant theory that is both *comprehensive and democratic*. It is compatible with scientific inquiry, the humanistic values of the democratic ethic, and the cultivation of the mind. Dewey's theory is humanistic, generous in spirit, yet suffused with the tough-mindedness of science.

The best source of a sound theory is philosophy, understood within the context of history and clearly linked to fundamental issues of practice. I believe that the history of educational research shows that no collection of theoretically unmoored research studies— often built on a false sense of precision through quantification— has ever led to a testable, comprehensive, democratic theory of education.

Psychological and sociological studies have not led to a comprehensive theory compatible with democratic and intellectual values. Many of these studies are useful, but they have not created a robust theory of education.

Broad social theories, such as Marxism, have not led to a comprehensive, democratic theory of education, though they have generated much writing on the subject.

Education is not primarily about technique. It's not about teaching technique, managerial technique, or research technique. These activities have value only insofar as they serve the essential purpose of education, which is the cultivation of democratic values and the cultivation of the mind. Absent the horizon-to-horizon reach of a comprehensive, democratic theory, technique wanders in a forest of incoherent empirical facts, no matter how many millions of dollars in grant money schools of education devour to raise their prestige ratings.

Today, these ancillary "fields" of teaching technique, managerial technique, and research technique dominate education in the universities. The democratic and intellectual ends of education are tragically ignored. How much—even in crude dollars—is this lack of a comprehensive theory costing us in lost brain power among the poor? Millions? Billions? More?

Schools of education should be teaching Deweyan theory, with the social sciences, humanities, and education serving as springboards for richer questions to explore and as critical frames for the theory itself. Let's scrap fragmented research programs in favor of pursuing theoretical and practical coherence.

I believe that too many public school leaders revert to technique rather than to ideas when they face a practical problem. This is the story of the profession's gutless, incoherent response to 60 years of planned attacks on all major social programs, including public basic and higher education. This cannot continue if we are to preserve our democracy.

Even Barack Obama gets an amnesia attack when education is the topic. In his great Philadelphia speech on race, he speaks against trivial distractions that obstruct serious political discourse and says, "Not this time. This time we want to talk about the crumbling schools that are stealing the future of black children and white children and Asian children and Hispanic children and Native American children. This time we want to reject the cynicism that tells us that these kids can't learn."

One would never know from Mr. Obama's statement that between 1820 and 1920 the children of more than 30 million Poles, Italians, Jews, and Germans learned English and democratic values in American public schools.[18] No expensive private school would dare tarnish its reputation by educating the ethnically blemished. Mr. Obama's education advisers are doing America harm by not educating him on the critical role public schools play in the democratization of immigrants to this day.

No private system of schools enrolls millions of poor children who speak little English. When will our governors, presidents, legislators—and public school teachers themselves—understand that the humble public school is one of the greatest democratic inventions in the world.

Henry Steele Commager, a great American historian, quotes Mary Antin, who arrived in America as a child. "Education was free," Antin writes, "the one thing [my father] was able to promise us . . . surer, safer than bread and shelter . . . . the freedom of the schools of Boston! No application to make, no questions asked, no examinations, rulings, exclusions; no machinations, no fees. The door stood open to everyone of us."[19]

Not one idea in Mr. Obama's statement can withstand the academic scrutiny of mainstream social scientists or informed educators. Mr. Obama's statement might sound good to his education advisors who think that "multiculturalism" is a comprehensive education theory rather than a slogan (which fits nicely, by the way, under the more substantive category of democracy).

Mr. Obama's unfortunate statement is strong evidence of the effectiveness of 60 years of propaganda against public basic and higher education and the interests of the poor and working class. When a liberal presidential candidate mouths the attack ideas of the radical Right against public education, is this not reasonable proof that our "strategy" of being the quiet mice in this society has killed our voice even within the councils of the Democratic Party? Who speaks with political power and conviction for public education across the decades? No one.

3. DEFEND PUBLIC SCHOOLS

Teacher unions and organizations of professional educators—at both the national and state levels—must mount a vigorous and clear-headed campaign to defend a great American institution against the false charge that public schools are failing, leveled by those I refer to as the Mystic Monks of the Market. This charge is blatant propaganda pushed by the economic elite to discredit public investment that helps ordinary citizens. And teacher unions and the profession in general let it pass like any other casual remark. This is not prudent behavior.

The charge is nonsense, but it is clearly hurtful. The threat of school privatization hangs heavy in our political air like smog in Beijing. We already have Edison Schools and charter schools, some run by profitmaking companies that take multimillion-dollar bites out of city education budgets.

Consider this possibility: imagine Wal-Mart or a billion-dollar hedge fund running a huge network of selective, undemocratic schools in America. Today, teachers are among the few middle-class toilers with decent jobs. When the Wal-Marters arrive, this private, cost-cutting money machine will have you, the teacher, working for $12 an hour with no benefits, a single-year contract, and no union representation.

It is imperative that the teacher unions initially organize an aggressive $50-million national and regional media campaign to tell the public and politicians the democratic success story of public education. The crudeness of that invidious media phrase, "our failing public schools," should be the first target of any such bold PR campaign.

If half the teachers in America contributed $20 each, a total war chest of more than $30 million would be available. Perhaps the Rockefeller or Carnegie foundations or Warren Buffett would throw in an additional $50 million. All it would take to get the ball rolling is a little out-of-the-box leadership.

You can be sure that the enemies of public education would not have sleepwalked through 60 years of ill-founded attacks. They would have fought like starving bears. Let's give public education the kind of warm and nurturing environment that the singleminded capitalists give themselves. Now *there* is a reform idea!

4. DEFUSE THE SOCIAL DYNAMITE IN OUR LARGE CITIES

In 1961 a conservative scientist and university president warned Americans of a danger more threatening to democracy than Iraq was when we invaded: "Social dynamite is building up in our...

cities in the form of unemployed out-of-school youth, especially in the Negro slums. We need accurate and frank information [on this condition] neighborhood by neighborhood."

A page later James B. Conant speaks directly to this democratic failure when he says that he has "sought to create a sense of anxious thoughts" in the minds of good citizens who live in the suburbs but who work in the cities. Conant imparts this thought: "To improve the work of slum schools requires an improvement in the lives of families who inhabit the slums. . . . but without a drastic change in the employment prospects for urban Negro youth, relatively little can be accomplished. . . . we need to know the facts, and when these facts indicate a dangerous social situation the American people should be prepared to take prompt action before it is too late."[20]

The school achievement of minority students, Conant says with uncommon sense, and their ability to work can come *only from the improvement of their family* and, I would add, their community lives. If, in 1961, we had started a two-generation "education for democratic citizenship" program to bring most of our poor families into the working and middle class, it is possible that by today, 50% to 70% of the children from formerly poor families would be achieving at or beyond grade level in our public schools, as middleclass children have always achieved in public schools. We chose instead to do nothing *significant* about family poverty and high minority dropout rates. By ignoring the morality of the democratic ethic, we chose to create an army of more than one million alienated youth annually, youth who are tenuously attached to school, work, family, and community.[21]

Is it sensible domestic or national security policy to dump one million undereducated and unemployed youth on the cold streets of our cities and towns every year? Does this human dumping accord with the morality of the democratic ethic?

A few years after Conant's warning about "social dynamite building in our cities," Los Angeles and Detroit were in flames. Must we wait for a second rebellion in these times of acute economic, political, and international stress—times that may mark the unraveling of American supremacy—before we discover the moral and social power of the democratic ethic, a power abused by both political parties since the 1980s?

---

1. *Democracy at Risk: The Need for a New Federal Policy in Education* (Washington, D.C.: Forum for Education and Democracy, April 2008), p. iii.

2. Robert B. Reich, *Supercapitalism: The Transformation of Business, Democracy, and Everyday Life* (New York: Borzoi Books, 2007), pp. 134-35.

3. Jonathan Kozol, "The Big Enchilada," *Harper's Magazine*, August 2007.

4. Jonathan Zimmerman, *Whose America? Culture Wars in the Public Schools* (Cambridge, Mass.: Harvard University Press, 2002), pp. 88-90, 97-98.

5. David Berliner, "If the Underlying Premise for No Child Left Behind Is False, How Can That Act Solve Our Problems" paper presented to the Iowa Academy of Education, Des Moines, 2004, pp. 7, 9.

6. Jared M. Diamond, *Collapse: How Societies Choose to Fail or Succeed* (New York: Viking, 2005).

7. Richard A. Gibboney, "Reforms's Green Fields," in idem, *The Stone Trumpet: A Story of Practical School Reform, 1960-1990* (Albany: State University Press of New York, 1994), p. 75.

8. Reich, p. 12.

9. Duncan K. Foley, *Adam's Fallacy: A Guide to Economic Theology* (Cambridge, Mass.: Belknap Press of Harvard University Press, 2006), p. 224.

10. Reich, p. 12.

11. Edward N. Wolff, *Top Heavy: A Study of Increasing Inequality of Wealth in the United States* (New York: Twentieth Century Fund, 2002), Figure 3.4, p. 14.

12. Henry Louis Gates, Jr., "Forty Acres and a Gap in Wealth," Op-ed, *New York Times*, 18 November 2007, p. 14.

13. "U.S. Data Show Rapid Minority Growth," New York Times, 1 June 2007, p. A-21.

14. Orlando Patterson, *The Ordeal of Integration: Progress and Resentment in America's "Racial" Crisis* (Washington, D.C.: Civitas/Counterpoint, 1998), p. 186-87.

15. David L. Kirp, *The Sandbox Investment: The Preschool Movement and Kids-First Politics* (Cambridge, Mass.: Harvard University Press, 2007), pp. 228-31.

16. Ibid., pp. 231-33.

17. Joseph E. Stiglitz, *The Roaring Nineties* (New York: Norton, 2003), p. 317.

18. Robert L. Church and Michael W. Sedlak, *Education in the United States: An Interpretive History* (New York: Free Press, 1976).

19. Henry Steele Commager, "Our Schools Have Kept Us Free," *Life*, 16 October 1950, pp. 46-47.

20. James Bryant Conant, *Slums and Suburbs: A Commentary on Schools in Metropolitan Areas* (New York: McGraw-Hill, 1961), pp. 146-47.

21. Christopher B. Swanson, *Cities in Crisis: A Special Analytic Report on High School Graduation* (Bethesda, Md.: Editorial Projects in Education Research Center, 2008), Section 1.

Note from author: My point of view in this Manifesto has been informed by John Dewey's philosophy, particularly his classic *Democracy and Education: An Introduction to the Philosophy of Education* (New York: Macmillan, 1916). *Democracy and Education* is a book whose democratic spirit honors both intelligence and ordinary human experience. I regret that its power as a theory of education has been lost to generations of educators who have not the patience to deal with its brilliant ideas and its complex (if sometimes turgid) academic style.

In the spirit of practice and Dewey's respect for "ordinary experience," I want to list four books that speak more directly to the creative demands of "doing" progressive teaching than the Manifesto offered: Richard A. Gibboney with Clark Webb, *What Every Great Teacher Knows* (Brandon, Vt.: Holistic Education Press, 1998); Deborah Meier, *The Power of Their Ideas* (Boston: Beacon Press, 1995); Nel Noddings, *When School Reform Goes Wrong* (New York: Teachers College Press, 2007); and Laurel N. Tanner, *Dewey's Laboratory School: Lessons for Today* (New York: Teachers College Press, 1997).

Schooling for Democracy*

By Nel Noddings

Students need to understand that going to college is not the only valuable path they can pursue. Once they learn to respect other choices, they are on their way to participating in the kind of democracy Dewey envisioned, in which people from all walks of life work together for the common good.

> *Most of the job openings in the next decade will be in occupations that do not require a college education.*

Current efforts at school reform—ostensibly designed to increase equality of outcomes—may actually be undermining our democracy by undervaluing the wide range of talents required in 21st-century America. I contend that, instead of insisting on more and

Nel Noddings is Lee L. Jacks Professor of Child Education, Emerita at Stanford University. Her latest book is *When School Reform Goes Wrong* (Teachers College Press, 2007).

* Permission to reprint granted by the author, Nel Noddings, and the publisher, Phi Delta Kappa International.

more standardization, we should be increasing variety, flexibility, and choice in what we offer in our schools.

A REALITY CHECK

Many policy makers today argue that all students should have a standard curriculum that will prepare them for "college or work." There is little debate about how preparation for these very different futures might also differ. Instead, more and more schools (and even some whole states) now require all secondary students to take traditional academic programs. The idea is to combat "the soft bigotry of low expectations" and prepare all students for college.

The irony here is that, where such bigotry existed, it still exists. But now it has been transformed into the bigotry of phony academic courses. Students are enrolled in, say, algebra, but the course they actually experience has only a vague resemblance to real algebra. When kids complete such courses, they have "algebra" on their transcripts, but they often have to take *prealgebra* in a community college. They have not "had" algebra; they've gone through a pseudo-algebra course. Why? Because "these kids can't handle a real algebra course."

Sometimes there is bigotry involved in this kind of response, but often it is simply the truth. Lots of kids are neither prepared for nor interested in academic courses in mathematics. In trying too hard to keep such students from failing, conscientious teachers deliver a course largely devoid of genuine mathematics. A few imaginative, energetic teachers manage to pull some unprepared youngsters up to a respectable level of performance, but even the best teachers often sacrifice the quality of their courses to spare their students the experience of failure.

But it is this system—not the teachers—that is failing our kids. An enlightened school would spend time finding out what the students are interested in and providing relevant courses. Kids who are forced into "rigorous" academic courses are doubly cheated: they do poorly in the required courses, and they are deprived of courses in which they might do well.

Do I seem to be defending tracking? Certainly, I'm not defending tracking as it has been implemented over the last century, but I enthusiastically endorse the concept. Schools should provide a variety of programs to address different needs, talents, and interests. Indeed, the comprehensive high school introduced in the early 20th century—for all its faults—made it possible to increase high school attendance from about 7% at the beginning of the century to well over 50% by mid-century. This was an unparalleled achievement in schooling.

Unfortunately, differentiated programs—that is, tracks—were conceived hierarchically; the "best" was the academic track, others were thought to be "lower," and the vocational track was judged to be "lowest" of all. To make matters worse, students were tested or evaluated on the basis of elementary school grades and were then *assigned to* the tracks. Thus, much to our shame, students who had demonstrable talent in mechanics or business were shunted into courses that were often poorly conceived, poorly taught, and largely held in contempt. This way of treating kids had to end, but the answer should not have been the one we have chosen: force everyone into the track once deemed "best."

I do not claim that all vocational courses have been of low quality. Many have been excellent.[1] It is clear also that most of the goals we now hold for values and attitudes can be included in vocational as well as academic courses. The courses to be eliminated or drastically improved are those that have been regarded as dead ends, as dumping grounds for students thought to be incapable of academic work.

Think how different it would be if students, with guidance and encouragement, could choose their own tracks and switch tracks if they felt they needed to. Think what school might be like if every course were challenging and well taught. The last two years of high school in a vocational/commercial track could be very much like two years of community college preparation for an occupation. Too many students now drop out (or are pushed out) of high school, and some who complete academic courses are not really prepared for college. Even some who complete college find themselves in jobs that do *not* require a college education, do not interest them, or both.

These observations lead us to another encounter with reality. According to the U.S. Bureau of Labor Statistics, most of the job openings in the next decade will be in occupations that do not require a college education. Although it is true that fields in the "knowledge world" are growing rapidly, the actual number of jobs in those areas is still far lower than the number needed in the service sector. In fact, it is predicted that there will be about five times as many jobs in the service sector that do not require a college education as there will be in the rapidly growing area of technology. Among the occupations offering the greatest number of jobs today are retail sales clerks, cashiers, office clerks, janitors and cleaners, food preparation workers, laborers and material movers, and waiters and waitresses.

High school students should be well informed about the job situation. They should also learn something about opportunities in the trades and in tech jobs that require some postsecondary training. If what is now mainly confined to postsecondary training could be offered in high school, that would be even better. Kids would have good reason to stay in school, and they would graduate ready for decent jobs.

Critics of this plan object that high schoolers are not mature enough to make crucial decisions about their occupational futures. Suppose a boy chooses a vocational track, loses interest, and decides that he would like to go to college. Critics of differentiated courses react to the possibility as if the boy's future is now hopelessly lost. The practical, ethical solution to this problem is to allow him to switch tracks. The decision might require as much as an extra year or two of high school, but that should be widely accepted. He is not being held back by punitive retention policies but by his own desire to gain more preparation. There is nothing sacred about the custom of finishing high school in exactly four years. We should also keep in mind that flexibility is a quality to be cultivated in the work force. Many people today change jobs often, and some make major moves across occupations. We can help young people prepare for the changing workplace by encouraging responsible choice and promoting the desire to continue to learn.

UNDERMINING DEMOCRACY

The idea that forcing everyone into a standard academic curriculum promotes democracy is highly questionable. It is not the idea of democracy celebrated by John Dewey and Walt Whitman. Dewey told us that democracy is "more than a form of government; it is primarily a mode of associated living, of conjoint communicated experience."[2] People from all walks of life, from all occupations, must work together for the common good. We must find ways to communicate effectively with one another.

We live in an interdependent society. In many of my talks, I have recommended that teachers take their middle school students on a field trip around their own town or city. What do they see people doing? The students should return to the school with a lengthy list of occupations upon which we all depend. Then let the students hear at least part of Whitman's "Song for Occupations"—a lovely, ringing affirmation of everyday life and the people who live it.[3] After hearing the poem, students might try writing their own (much shorter) songs to occupations. Whitman reminds readers of what it should mean to live in a democracy, of how we should value one another.

Too often in our schools today, kids hear the message (spoken or implied) that they should "go to college or be nothing." According to a recent front-page article in the *New York Times*, several urban school districts in the South have now proudly eliminated their programs that are not college preparatory.[4] They are determined to prepare all of their students for college, even though they are having a hard time getting many of their students through high school. Advocates of universal college attendance contend that a college degree is necessary for admission to the middle class. If that were so, 75% of our current citizens would now be living below the middle class. The crucially important goal for today's urban secondary schools should be to keep kids in school until they get a diploma. With that diploma in hand, they may feel confident enough to pursue some form of postsecondary training—possibly, but not necessarily, college.

The message "Go to college" is sent with good intentions; it is meant to inform students that they can all "make it" if they work hard. But it is a nasty, antidemocratic message. It undervalues large numbers of our citizens who do work on which we all depend. Those kids who do not want to go to college are demeaned. Many who force themselves into college, though their talents lie elsewhere, will quickly drop out, and those who go to college and succeed may not appreciate the work and intelligence of those who do not go.[5] Indeed, they may complete college with the notion that those who did not go had the opportunity and blew it. Their lower place on the economic ladder is, therefore, deserved. With an adequate education for democratic life, these privileged young people would understand that we live in a thoroughly interdependent society and that no person who works full time at an honest job should live in poverty. Instead of concentrating on this message, we divide our kids into winners and losers and pretend that, by "preparing" them all for college, we can make them all winners. We are on the wrong track.

In our efforts to prepare students for life in a democracy, we put great emphasis on learning facts about voting, our institutions of government, and the history of our nation, but we do little to help them appreciate the sort of democracy envisioned by Whitman and described by Dewey. Dewey wanted us to perfect the arts of communication that sustain a democratic mode of associated living. If we can do this, he wrote, "democracy will come into its own, for democracy is a name for a life of free and enriching communion. It had its seer in Walt Whitman. It will have its consummation when free social inquiry is indissolubly wedded to the art of full and moving communication." [6]

Dewey had in mind the full range of communicative arts—poetry, music, fine arts, literature, language, dance—and he tried to show how these can work with and contribute to social inquiry. If we were to take his recommendations seriously, we would stop stuffing facts into our students and give them time to investigate social/political issues, share their findings with classmates, and express themselves through the artistic mode of their choice. And notice that these activities can be done in vocational, commercial, or academic classes. [7]

Another move we should make to restore interest in democratic life is to expand the range of topics explored in each course. Many of us have discussed teaching the "whole child" at the elementary school level, but we rarely consider what this might look like at the high school level. [8] Our teaching at that level should help students understand that there is more to life than earning and spending money. Adolescents need to explore and discuss such great existential topics as faith, immortality, happiness, love, character, suffering, and morality. By expanding the disciplines from within—yes, even math—we can address some of these topics.

Adolescents also need to consider important personal and social issues. We can hardly expect them to become critical thinkers if they are not invited to discuss controversial issues. Consider these: If young people join the military and engage in combat, might they lose their moral identity? How does this happen? Why are we so influenced by advertising? Why, even though we do not believe the message, does advertising work? Are the days of gender discrimination over? Should women continue to enter the "caring" professions? Why are those professions so poorly paid? Is religion a force for good or evil in the world? Why are outspoken atheist writers now so often on the bestseller lists? Do we have moral obligations to nonhuman animals? What are they? All of these questions and many others are central to the maintenance and enhancement of democratic life in the 21st century. They should be vigorously discussed in our high schools, for the young people in our schools will live the remainder of their lives in this new century.

There are also questions of everyday life that need to be addressed. What does it mean to make a home? Why should people be homeless? What do people suffer in exile? What is the meaning of friendship? How is it expressed? What do parents owe their children? What practices are considered best for parenting in a postindustrial society?[9]

The underlying idea of the comprehensive high school is worth preserving, analyzing, revising, and extending. The idea is to educate all adolescents, regardless of their eventual occupations, for life in a democratic society. We may—and I argue that we should—provide different courses to meet different needs and interests, but we should also bring students from different programs together in student government and in a wide range of extracurricular activities. Today, we give far too little attention to the possible contributions of extracurricular activities. In some cities, we provide magnet schools or schools that serve particular occupational interests, but this practice overlooks the importance of encouraging students with widely varying interests and talents to *work together* in governing their school, launching projects, and developing attitudes toward the healthy use of leisure time. And in doing so, we overlook the central idea of democracy as a mode of associated living.

Within each program, teachers and students should strive for excellence, but excellence should not be defined in terms of grade-point average or the number of Advanced Placement courses taken. Excellence is rightly defined in the context of particular endeavors, but it should be appreciated across the entire society. John Gardner had it right when he said:

> An excellent plumber is infinitely more admirable than an incompetent philosopher. The society that scorns excellence in plumbing because plumbing is a humble activity and tolerates shoddiness in philosophy because it is an exalted activity will have neither good plumbing nor good philosophy. Neither its pipes nor its theories will hold water.[10]

Gardner pointed out that there are many opportunities for post-secondary training and that "the young person who does not go on to college should be enabled to look forward to just as active a period of growth and learning . . . as does the college youngster."[11] But Gardner did not see it as the responsibility of secondary schools to prevent the hopeless feeling of failure that many students today experience in our high schools. Instead, he suggested, "What they must be helped to recognize is that there are many kinds of further learning outside of formal high school and college programs. The fact that they have not succeeded in high school simply means that they must continue their learning in other kinds of situations." [12]

But youngsters who fail repeatedly in their school years are likely to reject opportunities for further learning. The task for us is to provide the variety of programs that will give the most kids a chance of achieving success, if not excellence. This will not be accomplished by forcing all students into academic programs regarded as prestigious. The current corruption of these courses is the very possibility that worried Gardner and should worry us all. It is shoddiness in an "exalted activity." Not only should we admire excellent plumbers in our adult society, we must also respect the students who will become plumbers and offer them genuine educational opportunities. Not everyone needs to go to college, but everyone needs and deserves a genuine education.

---

1. See Mike Rose, *Possible Lives: The Promise of Public Education in America* (Boston: Houghton Mifflin, 1995); see also W. Norton Grubb, ed., *Education Through Occupations in American High Schools*, 2 vols. (New York: Teachers College Press, 1995).

2. John Dewey, *Democracy and Education* (New York: Macmillan, 1916), p. 87.

3. Walt Whitman, *Poetry and Prose* (New York: Library of America, 1982).

4. See Sara Rimer, "Urban Schools Aiming Higher Than Diploma," *New York Times*, 17 January 2008, pp. A-1, 22.

5. On the intelligence of workers, see Mike Rose, *The Mind at Work: Valuing the Intelligence of the American Worker* (New York: Penguin, 2005). See also Mike Rose, "Intelligence, Knowledge, and the Hand/ Brain Divide," *Phi Delta Kappan*, May 2008, pp. 632-39.

6. John Dewey, *The Public and Its Problems* (New York: Henry Holt, 1927), p. 184.

7. See Nel Noddings, *When School Reform Goes Wrong* (New York: Teachers College Press, 2007).

8. See the September 2005 special issue of *Educational Leadership* devoted to The Whole Child.

9. These questions are discussed in Nel Noddings, *Critical Lessons: What Our Schools Should Teach* (Cambridge: Cambridge University Press, 2006).

10. John W. Gardner, *Excellence* (1961; reprint, New York: Norton, 1984), p. 102.

11. Ibid.

12. Ibid., p. 103.

Strong Schools Are Essential For Democracy*

By Deborah Meier

Some believe that defense of public education is merely a "special interest issue." For a minority, it's a matter of principle that private, for-profit companies are better than public institutions regardless of results. The others would dispense with the public schools if any alternative could produce higher test scores or reduce the gap between the scores of whites and blacks. In fact, some critics of public education claim that reducing the test score gap is the civil

---

Deborah Meier is a senior scholar and adjunct professor at New York University's Steinhardt School of Education, a board member and director of New Ventures at Mission Hill, director and advisor to the Forum for Democracy and Education, and a member of the board of the Coalition of Essential Schools. She lives in Hillsdale, N.Y.

rights issue of our time, as well as the cure for our economic ills. They claim that anything that distracts us from focusing on these two issues undermines both the poor and the rich simultaneously. It can be an irresistible argument—if you don't think about it.

While outright calls for privatization in the form of vouchers remain unpopular, privatization by any other name is widespread. Both not-for-profit and forprofit private organizations now operate publicly funded schools in many states. Even if there is no evidence that such privatization solves either the test score gap or the nation's economic woes, the critics of public schools tell us that it is always worth a try. In fact, they keep telling us that we should stop "wasting" tax dollars on public education and use that money for various privatization schemes. Thus, the line between public and private becomes harder and harder to find.

Under these circumstances, it is a pleasure to read Richard Gibboney's manifesto on behalf of public schooling's traditional democratic mission. Starting with two quotes from the outrageous Thomas Paine and strewn with old-fashioned (not an insult) critiques of unchecked capitalism, his manifesto is loud, sometimes brash, occasionally inaccurate, and a delight to read.

Arthur C. Brooks, the new president of the decidedly right-wing American Enterprise Institute, notes that "despite the rise in government spending between 1972 and 2002 . . . the percentage of Americans who said they were happy . . . 30% . . . did not change." Ergo, he argues, government can "only make things worse if they tried . . . through taxation and public spending."[1] Brooks may not have noticed that it was precisely by means of government policy that the rich got richer and the poor got poorer in the past 20 years. Perhaps that increasing disparity in wealth accounts for why the rate of government spending to happiness has not changed. He doesn't ask about the happiness gap between rich and poor, but maybe that hasn't changed either. Would Brooks change his mind if it had?

But one thing is clear, government spending—local, state, or federal—is not how conservatives hope to improve education. "Throwing" money at the schools is a waste, especially when there's a "real" war to fight. Thus AEI scholars show a lack of concern over spending in Iraq, but they begrudge every penny spent in the war against ignorance.

Unfair? After all, many AEI scholars and supporters have been eager beavers for the No Child Left Behind Act, though they were far from eager when it was the Elementary and Secondary Education Act, which they saw as just "throwing money." These scholars also do not seem disturbed at increased mayoral and state control of urban schools, which, in other cases, they would call the "state's heavy hand." They don't mind "big government" when it helps reinforce their biases in favor of the free marketplace and morality. In fact, they applaud policies that hope to change behavior through punishment. For example, conservatives favor grade-retention policies although they certainly show no evidence of improving even test scores, and there is ample evidence that these policies increase the dropout rate among the poor. But these policies, along with a host of zero-tolerance policies that have swept over schools, appeal to conservatives as proper punishment for failure.

POVERTY HANDICAPS CHILDREN

The handicaps poor children start with are not merely that they have, statistically, less of most things, but that they also have more of the wrong things. They are more restless, more independent, etc. They talk a lot but say the wrong things. Test scores can reflect race and class and can do so for even very young students. This is not the place to pursue this subject in detail, but testing is the best and surest way to create a system for maintaining gaps. It should be no surprise that we are seeing more tracking, perhaps most insidiously in the form of different schools for different kids, often under the name of choice. It's not possible that the inventors of these policies were unaware of this.

Gibboney is too hard on the National Education Association and the American Federation of Teachers. They have two faults. First, they probably reflect their membership's ambivalence and fearfulness. Second, they have been deserted by a weakened labor movement in general, and there now are fewer liberal allies, which makes it riskier to be militant. I think, like Gibboney, that unions should be bolder, but I'm sitting on the sidelines saying this. The teachers unions also might be wiped out if they try to be more militant.

But Gibboney is completely right that few educators, and even fewer noneducators, see any of these issues as serious policy questions. Only the claim that it is public schools that are undermining our economy gets any national exposure. As a result, even those who find the economic argument both morally and factually nonsense are sometimes grateful. Some attention might be better than none.

Even if the argument connecting student test scores and corporate profits were true, it is a weak argument for doing something right now. A rush to improve scores on the part of those at the bottom would take far more time than the naysayers claim we have. Changes in schooling take five to 15 years. During this time, our competitors will be raising their scores too. After all, many large American-based corporations and foundations, such as Microsoft, are subsidizing the school systems of our competitors.

> *Strong schools upheld and honored by their own constituents in every community in America are one bulwark of democracy.*

If inequality in test scores is bad for the economy (though it's not true for China, for example), what about inequality of medical care? Where does the corporate elite stand on that? Or inequality in housing? Or inequality in preschool child care, summer experiences for children, or prison sentencing? Or the inequality these critics do not mention, the inequality in income? Citizens in a more robust democracy would be asking such questions.

I'm ready to sign on to Gibboney's four recommendations. We need to do something about poverty. We need to do some deep thinking about the connection between democracy and schooling. We need public policy that strengthens, not weakens, unions. I don't know if there is a reason to expect "dynamite" in our cities, as Gibboney warns, but we certainly need a better urban policy.

Sometimes, I fear that the less said the better when it comes to school politics. But that's a short-sighted attitude that only speaks to how disabled the argument for democracy itself has become. Democracy has become one of those "process" issues that neither voters nor politicians want to take on, hoping that somehow our constitutional rights will hold up long enough without our reasoned and impassioned defense.

Strong schools upheld and honored by their own constituents in every community in America are one bulwark of democracy. The weaker schools become, the more dependent they are on mandates from above, such as test scores that shortchange what being well-educated means. When educating our kids for tomorrow falls beyond our shared responsibility, then democracy is already dead. Thanks, Richard Gibboney, for calling the alarm, even if we may not agree on what should be done next.

---

1. Patricia Cohen, "American Enterprise Institute Names a New President," *New York Times*, 15 July 2008, p. E2.

References

Aikin, W. M. (1942). *The story of the Eight-Year Study.* New York: Harper & Brothers.

Alexander, L., & James, H. T. (1987). *The nation's report card: Improving the assessment of student achievement.* Cambridge, MA: National Academy of Education.

Angier, N. (2008, November 11). Scientists and philosophers find that 'gene' has a multitude of meanings. *The New York Times,* D2.

Angoff, W. J. (Ed.). (1971). *The College Board admissions testing program: A technical report.* New York: College Entrance Examination Board.

Baird, L. L. (1985). Grades, tests, and accomplishments. *Research in Higher Education, 23*(1), 3-85.

Baker, K. (2007, October). Are international tests worth anything? *Phi Delta Kappan, 89*(2), 101-104.

Baker, R. (1983, April 30). Beset by mediocrity. *New York Times,* A23.

Baldi, S., Jin, Y., Skemer, M., Green, P. J., & Herget, D. (2007, December 4). *Highlights from PISA 2006: performance of U. S. 15-year-old students in science and mathematics literacy in an international context.* Washington, DC: National Center for Education Statistics. Retrieved from http://nces.ed.gov/pubsearch/pubsinfo.asp?pubid=2008016

Balta, V. (2002, October 25). End creative teaching, official says 'Assistant secretary: No waivers of No Child Left Behind.' *Stockton Record.* Retrieved from http://carrot.physics.buffalo.edu/archives/2002/10_2002/msg00490.html

Barber, B. R. (1995, April 19). Workshops of our democracy. *Education Week.* Retrieved from www.edweek.org/ew/articles/1995/04/19/30barb.h14.html?qs=barber+workshops

Barber, B. R. (1998). *A passion for democracy.* Princeton, NJ: Princeton University Press.

Barton, P. (2006). *High school reform and work: Facing labor market realities.* Princeton, NJ: Educational Testing Service. Retrieved from www.ets.org/Media/Research/pdf/PICHSWORK.pdf

Beaton, A. E., Mullis, I. V. S., Martin, M. O., Gonzalez, E. J., Kelly, D. L., & Smith, T. A. (1996a). *Mathematics achievement in the middle school years.* Chestnut Hill, MA: TIMSS International Study Center, Boston College.

Beaton, A. E., Mullis, I. V. S., Martin, M. O., Gonzalez, E. J., Kelly, D. L., & Smith, T. A. (1996b). *Science achievement in the middle school years.* Chestnut Hill, MA: TIMSS International Study Center, Boston College.

Bebchuk, L., & Fried, J. (2004). *Pay without performance: The unfulfilled promise of executive compensation.* Cambridge, MA: Harvard University Press.

Bell, T. H. (1988). *The thirteenth man: A Reagan memoir.* Old Tappan, NJ: Free Press.

Bennett, W. J. (2001, March). *The state and future of American education.* Speech to the Heritage Foundation on the 25th Anniversary of its founding.

Berliner, D. C. (2009, March). *Poverty and potential: Out-of-school factors and school success.* Boulder, CO & Tempe, AZ: Education and the Public Interest Center & Educational Policy Research Unit.

Berliner, D. C., & Biddle, B. J. (1995). *The manufactured crisis.* Reading, MA: Addison-Wesley Longman.

Bestor, A. (1953). *Educational wastelands: The retreat from learning in public schools.* Champaign, IL: University of Illinois Press.

Biancolli, A. (2001, April 27). At least our kids ask questions. *The Washington Post,* A23.

Bloomberg, M. (2007, December 31; 2008, January 7). A race we can all win. *Newsweek.* Retrieved from www.newsweek.com/id/81592/output/print

Booher-Jennings, J. (2005, Summer). Below the bubble: 'Educational triage' and the Texas accountability system. *American Educational Research Journal, (42)*2, 231-268.

Bowden, E., Jung-Beeman, M., Fleck, J., & Kounios, J. (2005, July). New approaches to demystifying insight. *TRENDS in Cognitive Sciences, (9)*7, 321-328.

Bracey, G. W. (1990, November 21). SAT scores: Miserable or miraculous? *Education Week,* 36.

Bracey, G. W. (1991, October). Why can't they be like we were? *Phi Delta Kappan, (73)*2, 104-117.

Bracey, G. W. (1999, October 17). The numbers game. *The Washington Post Book World,* X04.

Bracey, G. W. (2000a, October 25). The malevolent tyranny of algebra. *Education Week,* 47.

Bracey, G. W. (2000b, May). The TIMSS final year study and report: A critique. *Educational Researcher*, 4-11.

Bracey, G. W. (2002a, February). NCLB: A plan for the destruction of public education: Just say 'No.' Retrieved from www.nochildleft.com/2003/feb03no.html

Bracey, G. W. (2002b). *The war against America's public schools.* Boston: Allyn & Bacon.

Bracey, G. W. (2004a, Fall). The perfect law. *Dissent.* Retrieved from www.dissentmagazine. org/article/?article=318

Bracey, G. W. (2004b). *The seven deadly absurdities of No Child Left Behind.* Retrieved from www.nochildleft.com/2004/oct04absurd.html

Bracey, G. W. (2005, February 2). Education's groundhog day. *Education Week,* 38.

Bracey, G. W. (2006a, July/August). Believing the worst. *Stanford Magazine.* Retrieved from www.stanfordalumni.org/news/magazine/2006/julaug/features/nclb.html

Bracey, G. W. (2006b, May 21). Heard the one about the 600,000 Chinese engineers? *The Washington Post,* B01.

Bracey, G. W. (2006c). *Reading educational research: How to avoid getting statistically snookered.* Portsmouth, NH: Heinemann.

Brett, R. (2008, July 23). Rocky River Middle School principal David Root critical of emphasis on school tests. *Plain Dealer.* Retrieved from www.cleveland.com/brett/plaindealer/index.ssf?/base/opinion-0/1216801802121550.xml&coll=2

Carnevale, A. (2005, February 2). Education and the economy: If we're so dumb, why are we so rich? *Education Week,* 40.

Carnoy, M., Jacobsen, R., Mishel, L., & Rothstein, R. (2005). *The charter school dust-up: Examining the evidence on enrollment and achievement.* Washington, DC: Economic Policy Institute; New York: Teachers College Press.

Carson, C. C., Huelskamp, R. M., & Woodall, T. D. (1993, May/June). Perspectives on education in America. *Journal of Educational Research,* 259-310.

Cavanagh, S. (2008, July 30). Experts question Calif.'s algebra edict. *Education Week,* 1.

Center for Public Integrity. (2008). *Broken government: An examination of executive branch failures since 2000.* Retrieved from www.publicintegrity.org/investigations/broken_government/assets/pdf/Brogo-PDF_final.pdf

Clowes, G. A. (2000, November). Milwaukee celebrates 10 years of school choice. *School Reform News.* Retrieved from http://www.heartland.org/publications/school%20reform/article/10862/Milwaukee_Celebrates_10_Years_of_School_choice.html

Cohen, R. (1990, September 4). Johnny's miserable SAT's. *The Washington Post,* A19.

College Board. (1977). *On further examination.* New York: Author.

College Board. (1990). *College-bound seniors, 1990.* New York: Author.

College Board. (1996). *1996 college-bound seniors.* New York: Author. Retrieved from http://professionals.collegeboard.com/data-reports-research/sat/archived/1996

College Board. (2008). *2008 college-bound seniors: Total group profile report.* New York: Author. Retrieved from http://professionals.collegeboard.com/profdownload/Total_ Group_Report.pdf

Commission on Chapter 1. (1992). *Making schools work for children in poverty.* Washington, DC: Author.

Connor, S. (2003, December 8). Glaxo chief: Our drugs do not work on most patients. *The Independent.* Retrieved from www.independent.co.uk/news/science/glaxo-chief-our-drugs-do-not-work-on-most-patients-575942.html

Cremin, L. A. (1961). *The Transformation of the school: Progressivism in American education, 1876-1957.* New York: Alfred A. Knopf.

Cremin, L. A. (1990). *Popular education and its discontents.* New York: Harper & Row.

Dewey, J. (1916). *Democracy and education.* New York: Macmillan.

Dickson, P. (2001). *Sputnik: The shock of the century.* New York: Walker & Company.

Dillon, S. (2008, December 10). Math gains reported for U.S. students. *The New York Times.* Retrieved from www.nytimes.com/2008/12/10/education/10math,html?scp= 2&sq=timss@st=cse

Dillon, S. (2009, February 17). For education chief, stimulus means power, money and risk. *The New York Times.* Retrieved from http://www.nytimes.com/2009/02/17/ education/17educ.html?scp=1&sq=

Downey, D. B., von Hippel, P. T., & Hughes, M. (2008, July). Are 'failing' schools really failing? Removing the influence of nonschool factors from measures of school quality. *Sociology of Education,* 242-270.

Duffett, A., Farkas, S., & Loveless, T. (2008, June 18). *High-Achieving students in the era of No Child Left Behind.* Washington, DC: Thomas B. Fordham Institute. Retrieved from www.edexcellence.net/detail/news.cfm?news_id=732

Educational Testing Service. (2005, June 22). *ETS poll: Americans say high schools aren't challenging our students.* Princeton, NJ: Author.

Eisenhower, D. D. (1965). *The White House years: Waging peace, 1956-1961.* New York: Doubleday.

Elicker, P. (1958). Let's speak the truth about our schools. *NASSP Bulletin, 42,* 1-10.

Elley, W. P. (2002). *How in the world do students read?* Hamburg, Germany: International Association for the Evaluation of Education Achievement.

Emery, K., & Ohanian, S. (2004). *Why is corporate America bashing our public schools?* Portsmouth, NH: Heinemann.

Estes, J. (1964, December 4). Gifted boy finds his way. *Life,* 79-80.

Featherstone, J. (1967a, August 19). Schools for children: What's happening in British classrooms. *The New Republic,* 17-21.

Featherstone, J. (1967b, September 2). How children learn. *The New Republic,* 17-21.

Featherstone, J. (1967c, September 9). Teaching children to think. *The New Republic,* 15-19.

Fields, G. (2008, November 11). D.C. school chief scores gains, ruffles feathers. *The Wall Street Journal Online.* Retrieved from http://sec.online.wsj.com/article/SB122636956 488016241.html

Fine, B. (1943, April 4). Ignorance of U.S. history shown by college freshmen. *The New York Times,* 1.

Finn, C. E., & Ravitch, D. (1987). *What do our 17-year-olds know? A report on the first national assessment of history and literature.* New York: Harper & Row.

Finn, C. E., & Ravitch, D. (2007). *Beyond the basics: Achieving a liberal education for all children.* Washington, DC: Thomas B. Fordham Institute. Retrieved from www.edexcellence.net/doc/Beyond_The_Basics_Final.pdf

Flener, F. (2001, April 6). *A geometry course that changed their lives: The guinea pigs after 60 years.* Presentation to the National Council of Teachers of Mathematics, Orlando, FL. Retrieved from www.maa.org/editorial/knot/NatureOfProof.html

Frederiksen, N. (1984, March). The real test bias. *American Psychologist,* 193-202.

Gallagher, C. W. (2007). *Reclaiming assessment.* Portsmouth, NH: Heinemann.

Gardner, H. (1983). *Frames of mind.* New York: Basic Books.

Gardner, H. (1991). *The unschooled mind.* New York: Basic Books.

Gardner, H. (1999). *Intelligence reframed: Multiple intelligences for the 21st century.* New York: Basic Books.

Glanz, J. (2004, March 30). At the center of the storm over Bush and science. *The New York Times.* Retrieved from http://www.nytimes.com/2004/03/30/science/at-the-center-of-the-storm-over-bush-and-science.html?sec=sec=health&&fta=y

Glass, G. V. (2008). *Fertilizers, pills and magnetic strips: The fate of public education in America.* Charlotte, NC: Information Age Publishing.

Glickman, C. (2008, November 18). *The latest nation at risk report.* Washington, DC: The Forum for Education and Democracy. Retrieved from www.forumforeducation.org/blog/index.php?post=95

Glod, M. (2008, December 10). Scores on science test causing concern in U.S. *The Washington Post,* A10. Retrieved from www.washingtonpost.com/wp-dyn/content/article/2008/12/09/AR2008120901031.html

Goodkin, S., & Gold, D. G. (2007, August 27). The gifted children left behind. *The Washington Post,* A13.

Goodlad, J. (1979). *What schools are for.* Bloomington, IN: Phi Delta Kappa.

Goodlad, J. (1997). *In praise of education.* New York: Teachers College Press.

Goodpaster, A. J. (1957, October 9). *Memorandum of conference with the president, October 8, 1957, 8:30 a.m.* Retrieved from http://history.spacebusiness.com/sputnik/files/sputnik28.pdf

Graham, P. A. (2005). *Schooling America: How the public schools meet the nation's changing needs.* New York: Oxford University Press, USA.

Greenberg, D. (2007, December 11). No mystery why Americans shun science careers. *The Chronicle of Higher Education.* Retrieved from http://chronicle.com/review/brainstorm/greenberg/?pg=8

Greenwood, P. W., Mann, D., & McLaughlin, M. W. (1975, April). *Federal programs supporting educational change, Volume III: The process of change.* Santa Monica, CA: The RAND Corporation.

Grubb, W. N. (2007, October). Dynamic inequality and intervention: Lessons from a small country. *Phi Delta Kappan, 89*(2), 105-114.

Hand, F. C. (1965, September). The camel's nose. *Phi Delta Kappan,* 8-12.

Handel, M. J. (2005). *Worker skills and job requirements: Is there a mismatch?* Washington, DC: Economic Policy Institute. Retrieved from www.epi.org/content.cfm/book_worker_skills

Hansen, F. A. (1993). *Testing testing: Social consequences of the examined life.* Berkeley, CA: University of California Press.

Hanushek, E. (2005, February 2). Education and the economy: Our school performance matters. *Education Week,* 40.

Hechinger, F. (1967, July 30). Schools vs. riots. *The New York Times,* 138.

Heckman, J. (2008). Schools, skills, and synapses. *Economic Inquiry, 46*(3), 289-324.

Herndon, J. (1971). *How to survive in your native land.* New York: Simon & Schuster.

Holton, G. (2003, April 23). An insider's view of 'A Nation at Risk' and why it still matters. *The Chronicle of Higher Education, 49*(33). Retrieved from http://chronicle.com/free/v49/i33/33b01301.htm

Hoover, E. (2008, December 3). Testing service describes GRE's new measure of 'noncognitive qualities.' *The Chronicle of Higher Education.* Retrieved from www.chronicle.com/daily/2008/12/7931n.htm

Hopmann, S. T., Brinek, G., & Retzl, M. (2008). *PISA according to PISA.* Vienna: LIT Verlag; Piscataway, NJ: Rutgers University.

Institute for Management Development. (2008a). *The world competitiveness scoreboard 2008.* Lausanne, Switzerland: Author. Retrieved from www.imd.ch/research/publications/wcy/upload/scoreboard.pdf

Institute for Management Development. (2008b). *IMD world competitiveness yearbook.* Lausanne, Switzerland: Author. Retrieved from www.imd.ch/research/publications/wcy/index.cfm

Institute for Management Development. (2008c). *IMD world competitiveness yearbook 2008: How long will the US keep its leadership positions?* Lausanne, Switzerland: Author. Retrieved from www.imd.ch/news/2008-WCY-rankings.cfm

Jefferson, T. (1782). *Notes on the State of Virginia.* In S. J. Hammond, K. R. Harwick, & H. L. Labert (2007) *Classics of American Policital and Constitutional Thought, Volume I.* Indianapolis, IN: Hackett Publishing.

Jensen E. P. (2008, February). A fresh look at brain-based education. *Phi Delta Kappan, 89*(6), 409-417.

Johnson, A. (2007, November 27). Failing schools are hurt by transfers: Federal law allows parents to shift children to better ones in county. *South Florida Sun-Sentinel,* B1.

Kaminski, M. (2009, March 19). Educating Obama. *Forbes Magazine.* Retrieved from www.forbes.com/2009/03-19/obama-schools-reform-opinions-contributors-education.htm

Kaszuba, M., & Brunswick, M. (2008, February 25). House, Senate override a Pawlenty veto for the first time. *Minneapolis-St. Paul Star Tribune.* Retrieved from www.startribune.com/politics/state/15942557.html

Kirp, D. (2007, November 19). Nature, nurture, and destiny. *The American Prospect.* Retrieved from http://www.prospect.org/cs/articles?article=nature_nuture_and_destiny

Knight, E. W. (1952). *Fifty years of American education: A historical review and critical appraisal.* New York: The Ronald Press Company.

Kornhaber, M. (2001). Howard Gardner. In J. A. Palmer (Ed.), *Fifty modern thinkers on education, from Piaget to the present.* London: Routledge.

Kounios, J., Fleck, J., Green, D., Payne, L., Stevenson, J., Bowden, E., et al. (2008). The origins of insight in resting-state brain activity. *Neuropsychologia, 46,* 281-291.

Kreisberg, S. (1992). *Transforming power: Domination, empowerment and education.* Ithaca, NY: State University of New York Press.

Kridel, C. (n.d.). *Eight-Year Study—Purpose, Method, Results.* Stateuniversity.com. Retrieved from http://education.stateuniversity.com/pages/1947/Eight-Year-Study.html

Kridel, C., & Bullough, R. V. (2007). *Stories from the Eight-Year Study: Reexamining Secondary Education in America.* Albany, NY: State University of New York Press.

Lakoff, G. (2004). *Don't think of an elephant: Know your values and frame the debate—the essential guide for progressives.* White River Junction, VT: Chelsea Green.

Lehrer, J. (2008, July 28). The eureka hunt. *The New Yorker,* 40.

Lemann, N. (1999). *The big test: The secret history of the American meritocracy.* New York: Farrar, Strauss, & Giroux.

Lewis, M. (2009, April). Wall Street on the tundra. *Vanity Fair,* 140-147.

Life. (1958a, March 24). *Schoolboys point up a U.S. weakness.* Author, 26-37.

Life. (1958b, April 7). *The waste of fine minds.* Author, 89-95.

Lohr, S. (2008, November 29). Do we overrate basic research? *The New York Times.* Retrieved from www.nytimes.com/2008/11/30/business30ping.html?_r=1@scp=3&sq=%22steve%20lohr%22&st=cse

Loewen, J. W. (1995). *Lies my teacher told me: Everything your American history textbook got wrong.* New York: The New Press.

Lowell, L., & Salzman, H. (2007, October). *Into the eye of the storm: Assessing the evidence on science and engineering education, quality, and workforce demand.* Washington, DC: The Urban Institute. Retrieved from www.urban.org/UploadedPDF/411562_salzman_ Science.pdf

Lynch, E. F. (1912, January). Is our public school system a failure? *Ladies Home Journal,* 5-6.

Lynch, E. F. (1914). *Educating the child at home.* New York: Harper & Brothers Publishers.

Magnuson, K., & Waldfogel, J. (Eds.). (2008). *Steady gains and stalled progress: Inequality and the Black-White test score gap.* New York: Russell Sage Foundation.

Manzo, K. K. (2007, December 5). America idles on international reading test. *Education Week,* 11.

Manzo, K. K. (2008, December). Asians best U.S. students in math and science. *Education Week.* Retrieved from www.edweek.org/ew/articles/2008/12/09/16timss.h28. html?r=1373015076

Martin, C. P. (2005, February 17). *Nature or nurture?* Retrieved from http://oscar.virginia. edu/x5701.xml

Martin, J. (2007, February 17). Advocate condemns No Child Left Behind. *Evansville Courier & Press.* Retrieved from www.courierpress.com/news/2007/aug/03/advocate-condemns-no-child-left-behind

McCluskey, N. (2007, July 28). No standards left behind. *The Wall Street Journal,* A8.

McCurry, J. (2009, February 25). *Export slump deepens Japanese economic crisis.* Retrieved from http://www.guardian.co.uk/business/2009/feb/25/japanese-economic-crists-recession

McLaughlin, M. (1990, December). The RAND Change Agent study revisited: Macro perspectives and micro realities. *Educational Researcher, 19,* 11-16.

Miller, G. (2007, July 30). *Chairman Miller remarks on the future of the No Child Left Behind law.* Retrieved from www.house.gov/apps/list/speech/edlabor_dem/RelJul30N CLBSpeech.html

Miller, J. (1991, October 5). Report questioning 'crisis' in education triggers an uproar. *Education Week.* Retrieved from www.edweek.org/ew/articles/1991/10/09crisis.h11. html?qs=miller&520=kearns%20sandia

Molnar, A. (1996). *Giving kids the business: The commercialization of America's schools.* Boulder, CO: Westview Press.

Monastersky, R. (2007, September 21). The real science crisis: Bleak prospects for young scientists. *The Chronicle of Higher Education.*

Mullis, I. V. S., Martin, M. O., Beaton, A. E., Gonzalez, E. J., Kelly, D. L., & Smith, T. A. (1998). *Mathematics and science achievement in the final year of secondary school.* Chester Hill, MA: International Study Center, Boston College.

Mullis, I. V. S., Martin, M. O., & Foy, P. (2008). *TIMSS 2007 international mathematics report.* Chester Hill, MA: International Study Center, Boston College.

Mullis, I. V. S., Martin, M. O., Gonzalez, E. J., & Chrostowski, S. J. (2004). *TIMSS 2003 international mathematics report.* Chester Hill, MA: International Study Center, Boston College.

Mullis, I. V. S., Martin, M. O., Kennedy, A. M., & Foy, P. (2007). *IEA's progress in international reading literacy study in primary school in 40 countries.* Chester Hill, MA: International Study Center, Boston College.

Munday, L., & Davis, J. (1974). Varieties of accomplishment: Perspectives on the meaning of academic talent (Research Report No. 62). Iowa City, IA: American College Testing Program.

Nathan, J. (1996). *Charter schools: Creating hope and opportunity for American education.* San Francisco: Jossey-Bass.

National Academies. (2007). *Rising above the gathering storm.* Washington, DC: National Academies Press.

National Center for Education Statistics. (1999, February 26). *The TIMSS videotape classroom study: Methods and findings from an exploratory research project on eighth-grade mathematics instruction in Germany, Japan, and the United States.* Washington, DC: U.S. Department of Education. Retrieved from www.nces.ed.gov/pubsearch/pubinfo. asp?pubid=1999074

National Center for Education Statistics. (2003, April). *International comparisons of fourth-grade reading literacy: Findings from the Progress in International Reading Literacy Study (PIRLS) of 2001.* Washington, DC: U.S. Department of Education. Retrieved from www.nces.ed.gov/pubsearch/pubinfo.asp?pubid=2003073

National Center for Education Statistics. (2004, December 15). *America's charter schools: Results from the NAEP 2003 pilot study.* Washington, DC: U.S. Department of Education.

National Center for Education Statistics. (2005). *NAEP 2004 trends in academic progress.* Washington, DC: U.S. Department of Education. Retrieved from www.nces.ed.gov/ nationsreportcard/pdf/main2005/2005464.pdf

National Center for Education Statistics. (2007a, December 4). *Highlights from PISA 2006: Performance of U.S. 15-year-old students in science and mathematics literacy in an international context.* Washington, DC: U.S. Department of Education. Retrieved from www.nces.ed.gov/pubsearch/pubinfo.asp?pubid=2008016

National Center for Education Statistics. (2007b). *International comparisons in fourth-grade literacy.* Washington, DC: U.S. Department of Education. Retrieved from http://nces.ed.gov/pubs2004/pirlspub

National Center for Education Statistics. (2008a). *The condition of education, 2008: The contexts of elementary and secondary education.* Washington, DC: U.S. Department of Education. Retrieved from www.nces.ed.gov/programs/coe/2008/section4/table.asp?tableID=912

National Center for Education Statistics. (2008b). *The nation's report card: Reading 2007.* Washington, DC: U.S. Department of Education. Retrieved from www.nces.ed.gov/nationsreportcard/pdf/main2007/2001496.pdf

National Commission on Excellence in Education. (1983, April 26). *A nation at risk.* Washington, DC: U.S. Department of Education.

National Governors Association. (2006, December 3). *National groups co-host briefing on 2006 PISA results, issue joint statement.* Press release. Retrieved from http://www.nga.org/portal/site/nga/menuitem.be806d93bb5ee77eee28aca9501010a0/vgnextoid=39 5f3b42921a6110VgnVCM1000001a01010aRCRD&vgnextchannel=759b8f200536 1010VgnVCM1000001a01010aRCRD&vgnextfmt=print

National Public Radio. (2008, August 7). *Film marks balancing act between twin towers.* Retrieved from www.npr.org/templates/story/story.pho?storyid=93389812

National Scientific Council on the Developing Child. (2006). *Excessive stress disrupts the architecture of the developing brain.* Washington, DC: Author. Retrieved from www.developingchild.net/pubs/wp/Stress_Disrupts_Architecture_Developing_Brain.pdf

Nature. (2007, August 23). *Indentured Labour.* Retrieved from www.nature.com/nature/journal/v448/n7156/ful/448839b.html

Newman, A. (Ed.). (1978). *In defense of the American public school.* Berkeley, CA: Mc-Cutchan Publishing Corporation.

The New York Times. (1920). *Severe strain on credulity.* Unsigned editorial.

The New York Times. (1969, July 17). *A correction.* 20.

The New York Times. (2009). *Barak Obama's inaugural address.* Retrieved from www/nytimes.com/2009/01/20/us/politics/20text-obama.html

Nichols, S. L., & Berliner, D. C. (2007). *Collateral damage: How high-stakes testing corrupts America's schools.* Cambridge, MA: Harvard Education Press.

Nichols, S. L., & Berliner, D. C. (2008 May). Why has high-stakes testing so easily slipped into contemporary American life? *Phi Delta Kappan, 89*(9), 672-676.

Nocera, J. (2007, February 3). From raider to activist, but still Icahn. *The New York Times,* D1.

Office for National Statistics. (2008, October 10). *International productivity: Revised estimates for 2007.* Newport, United Kingdom: Author. Retrieved from www.statistics.gov.uk/cci/nugget.asp?id=160

Ohanian, S. (2008). *When childhood collides with NCLB.* Charlotte, VT: Vermont Society for the Study of Education.

Otto, M. (2007, February 28). For want of a dentist; Pr. George's boy dies after bacteria from tooth spread to brain. *The Washington Post,* B1.

Owen, D. (1985). *None of the above: Behind the myth of scholastic aptitude.* Boston: Houghton Mifflin.

Perlstein, L. (2007). *Tested: One American school struggles to make the grade.* New York: Henry Holt & Co.

Pear, R. (2005, February 27). Microsoft chairman challenges governors to improve high schools. *The New York Times.* Retrieved from www.nytimes.com/2005/02/27/education/27bill.html

Petrilli, M. (2008, July 17). *The genius of American education.* Retrieved from www.edexcellence.net/gadfly/index.cfm?issue=421#d25

Phillips, G. W. (2007). *Expressing international education achievement in terms of U. S. performance standards: Linking NAEP achievement levels to TIMSS.* Washington, DC: American Institutes for Research.

PISA. (2006). *PISA released items—reading.* Retrieved from www.pisa.oecd.org/dataoecd/13/34/38709396.pdf

Podesta, J. (2007, February 27). *Remarks on education report roll out.* Remarks made to U.S. Chamber of Commerce. Retrieved from www.americanprogress.org/issues/2007/02/podesta_education_remarks.html

Prais, S. J. (2008). England: Poor survey response and no sampling of teaching groups. In S. T. Hopmann, G. Brinek, & M. Retzl (Eds.). *Pisa According to Pisa.* Vienna: LIT Verlag; Piscataway, NJ: Transaction Publishers.

Ravitch, D. (2000). *Left back: A century of failed school reforms.* New York: Simon & Schuster.

Revkin, A. C. (2004, October 19). Bush vs. the laureates: How science became a partisan issue. *The New York Times.* Retrieved from http://www.nytimes.com/2004/10/19/science/19poli.html?_r=1

Richter, J. (2003, November 10). *New thinking on children, poverty & IQ.* Washington, DC: Connect for Kids. Retrieved from www.connectforkids.org/node/516

Robelen, E. (2008, May 21). NAEP gap continuing for charters. *Education Week,* 1.

Rotberg, I. (2008, June 11). Quick fixes, test scores, and the global economy. *Education Week,* 27.

Rothstein, R., Jacobsen, R., & Wilder, T. (2006, November 14). *'Proficiency for all' an oxymoron.* Washington, DC: Economic Policy Institute. Retrieved from www.epi.org/webfeatures/viewpoints/rothstein_20061114.pdf

Rouse, C. E. (2000). *School reform in the 21st century: A look at the effect of class size and school vouchers on the academic achievement of minority students.* Working Paper #440, Industrial Relations Section, Princeton University. Retrieved from www.irs.princeton.edu/pubs/pdfs/440.pdf

Salzman, H. (2007, November 6). *Globalization of R&D and innovation: Implications for U.S. STEM workforce and policy.* Testimony to the U. S. House of Representatives. Retrieved from www.urban.org/UploadedPDF/901129_salzman_stem_workforce.pdf

Salzman, H., & Lowell, L. (2008, May 1). Making the grade. *Nature,* 28-30.

Shaker, P., & Heilman E., (2008). *Reclaiming education for democracy.* New York: Routledge.

Shonkoff, J. P. (2006, November 5). A promising opportunity for developmental and behavioral pediatrics at the interface of neuroscience, psychology, and social policy: Remarks on receiving the 2005 C. Anderson Aldrich Award. *Pediatrics,* 2187-2191.

Shonkoff, J. P., & Phillips, D. (2000). *From neurons to neighborhoods: The science of early childhood development.* Washington, DC: National Research Council. Retrieved from www.nap.edu/openbook.php?isbn=0309069882

Silberman, C. (1970). *Crisis in the classroom.* New York: Random House.

Spring, J. (1976). *The sorting machine: National educational policy since 1945.* New York: David McKay.

Sternberg, R. J. (2006, February 22). The 'habit' of creativity and how to develop it. *Education Week,* 47.

Sternglass, E., & Bell, S. (1983, April). Fallout and SAT scores: Evidence for cognitive damage during early infancy. *Phi Delta Kappan,* 64(8), 539-545.

Teitelbaum, M. (1996, March 19). Too many engineers, too few jobs. *The New York Time.* Retrieved from www.xent.com/FoRK-archive/spring96/0303.html

Time. (1938, July 18). *Fifty-five authors*. Author. Retrieved from www.time.com/time/magazine/article/0,9171,760053,00.html?iid-chix-sphere

Tomsho, R. (2008, May 13). No Child Left Behind lacks bite: Worst-performing schools rarely adopt radical remedies. *The Wall Street Journal*. Retrieved from www.masfps.org/bert/20080513-WSJ_NCLB.Article.pdf

Toppo, G. (2008, December 9). U.S. students' math, science scores deliver mixed results. *USA Today*. Retrieved from www.usatoday.com/news/education/2008-12-09-math-sci-scores_N.htm

Tough, P. (2008). *Whatever it takes: Geoffrey Canada's quest to change Harlem and America*. New York: Houghton Mifflin.

Turkheimer, E., Haley, A., D'Onofrio, B., Waldron, M., & Gottesman, I. I. (2004). Socio-economic status modifies heritability of IQ in young children. *Psychological Science*, *14*, 623-628.

Tyler, R. (1976). *Perspectives on American education: Reflections on the past, challenges for the future*. Chicago: Science Research Associates.

U.S. Chamber of Commerce. (2007, February). *Leaders and laggards: A state by state report card on educational effectiveness*. Washington, DC: Author. Retrieved from www.uschamber.com/icw/reportcard/default

U.S. Department of Education. (2009). *The American recovery and reinvestment act of 2009: Saving and creating jobs and reforming education*. Retrieved from http://www.ed.gov/policy/gen/leg/recovery/implementation.html

U.S. Department of Labor. (1992). *Secretary's Commission on Achieving Necessary Skills*. Washington, DC: Author. Retrieved from http://wdr.doleta.gov/SCANS

U.S. News & World Report. (1956, November 30). We are less well educated than fifty years ago. Author, 68-82.

U.S. News & World Report. (1958, January 24). What went wrong with U.S. schools. Author, 68-77.

U.S. Office of Education. (1945). *Life adjustment education for every youth*. Washington, DC: Author.

University of Washington News. (2008, June 4). *Degrees Without Freedom: Masculinities and Unemployment in Northern India*. Press release for Jeffrey, C., Jeffery, P., & Jeffery, R. Palo Alto: Stanford University Press.

The Washington Post & Times Herald. (1957, November 10). *Von Braun sees more Soviet firsts*. Author, A1.

Wallis, C. (2008, 8 June). No Child Left Behind—Doomed to fail? *Time.* Retrieved from www.time.com/nation/article/0,8599,1812758,00.htm

Warren, R. J. (2008, May). *Graduation rates for choice and public school students in Milwaukee, 2003-2007.* Retrieved from www.schoolchoicewi.org/data/currdev_links/ Grad rates-2008-8.5x11.pdf

Weinstein, E. (n.d.). *How and why government, universities, and industry create domestic labor shortages of scientists and high-tech workers.* Unpublished paper. Retrieved from www. nber.org/~peat/PapersFolder/Papers/SG/NSF.html

Whittington, D. (1991). What have our 17-year-olds known in the past? *American Educational Research Journal, 28*(4), 759-780.

Wikipedia. (n.d.). *Competitiveness.* Author. Retrieved from http://en.wikipedia.org/wiki/ Competitivness

Willingham, D. (2008, February). When and how neuroscience applies to education. *Phi Delta Kappan, 89*(6), 421-423.

Willis, J. (2008, February). Building a bridge from neuroscience to the classroom. *Phi Delta Kappan, 89*(6), 424-427.

Wilson, S. (1958, March 24). It's time to close our circus. *Life*, 36-37.

World Economic Forum. (2007). *Global Competitiveness Report 2007-2008.* Davos, Switzerland: Author.

World Economic Forum. (2008). *Global competitiveness index rankings.* Davos, Switzerland: Author. Retrieved from www.weforum.org/pdf/gcr/2008/rankings.pdf

Wolfe, T. (1979). *The right stuff.* New York: Farrar, Strauss, & Giroux.

Yatvin, J. (2008, February). 2007 NCTE Presidential address: Where ignorant armies clash by night. *Research in the Teaching of English, 42*(3), 363-372.

Zakaria, F. (2006, January 9). We all have a lot to learn. *Newsweek.* Retrieved from http:// fareedzakaria.com/articles/newsweek/010906.html

Zimmer, C. (2008, November 11). Now: The rest of the genome. *The New York Times,* D1.

Subscriptions at a Glance

If you are looking for reliable preK-12 research to . . .

- tackle the challenges of NCLB;
- identify research-based teaching practices;
- make educationally sound and cost-effective decisions; and most importantly
- improve student achievement . . .

then look no further than an ERS Subscription.

Simply pick the subscription option that best meets your needs:

■ **School District Subscription**—a special research and information subscription that provides education leaders with timely research on priority issues in preK-12 education. All new ERS publications and periodicals, access to customized information services through the ERS special library, and 50 percent discounts on additional ERS resources are included in this subscription for one annual fee. This subscription also provides the entire administrative staff "instant" online, searchable access to the wide variety of ERS resources. You'll gain access to the ERS electronic library of more than 1,600 educational research-based documents, as well as additional content uploaded throughout the year.

■ **Individual Subscription**—designed primarily for school administrators, staff, and school board members who want to receive a personal copy of new ERS studies, reports, and/or periodicals published and special discounts on other resources purchased.

■ **Other Education Agency Subscription**—available for state associations, libraries, departments of education, service centers, and other organizations needing access to quality research and information resources and services.

Your ERS Subscription benefits begin as soon as your order is received and continue for 12 months. For more detailed subscription information and pricing, contact ERS toll free at 800-791-9308, by email at ers@ers.org, or visit us online at www.ers.org!

ORDER FORM FOR RELATED RESOURCES

Quantity	Item Number	Title	Base Price	ERS Individual Subscriber Discount Price	ERS School District Subscriber Discount Price	Total Price
				Price per Item		
	0760	*Education Hell: Rhetoric vs. Reality*	$30.00	$22.50	$15.00	
	0743	*Answering the Critics of School Administration, 2nd Ed.*	$30.00	$22.50	$15.00	
	0530	*Supporting School Improvement: Lessons from Districts Successfully Meeting the Challenge*	$28.00	$21.00	$14.00	
	0496	*Understanding and Using Education Statistics: It's Easier (and More Important) Than You Think, 2nd Ed.*	$20.00	$15.00	$10.00	
		Shipping and Handling** (Add the greater of $4.50 or 10% of purchase price.)				
		Express Delivery** (Add $20 for second-business-day service.)				
		**Please double for international orders.			TOTAL PRICE:	

SATISFACTION GUARANTEED! If you are not satisfied with an ERS resource, return it in its original condition within 30 days of receipt and we will give you a full refund.

Visit us online at www.ers.org for a complete listing of resources!

Method of payment:

☐ Check enclosed (payable to ERS)   ☐ P.O. enclosed (Purchase order #_____)

☐ MasterCard   ☐ VISA   ☐ American Express

Name on Card: _____ Credit Card #:_____

Expiration Date: _____ Signature: _____

Ship to: (please print or type)   ☐ Dr.   ☐ Mr.   ☐ Mrs.   ☐ Ms.

Name: _____ Position: _____

School District or Agency: _____ ERS Subscriber ID#: _____

Street Address: _____

City, State, Zip: _____

Telephone: _____ Fax: _____

Email: _____

Return completed order form to:
Educational Research Service • 1001 North Fairfax Street, Suite 500 • Alexandria, VA 22314-1587
Phone: 703-243-2100 • Toll Free Phone: 800-791-9308 • Fax: 703-243-1985 • Toll Free Fax: 800-791-9309
Email: ers@ers.org • Web site: www.ers.org